LOVE YOUR NEIGHBOR

A Biblical, Theological, Historical, and Sociological Perspective.

Ayad S. Attia

Copyright © 2022 by Ayad S. Attia
All rights reserved

Abstract

Throughout Arab history, fundamentalist tendencies have fostered distrust and prevented cooperation between Muslim and Christian Arabs. Sociologist and theologian Peter Berger demonstrates that such radicalization creates cognitive minorities, rendering these minorities unable to engage the other. The hypothesis of this project is that awareness of being a cognitive minority can be the first step to becoming open to facing the other. Three sessions were used to test cognitive minority awareness as a means to overcome relational division. Using the qualitative research method, the results show marginal change due to subsequent challenges when subjects returned to their respective communities.

Acknowledgement

First and foremost, my thanks go to United Theological Seminary for reaching out to me in God's providence and making so many incredible things possible. My life has been thoroughly transformed in the past five years.

This project would not have succeeded without the support and encouragement of various people. I am indebted to Dr. Wendy Deichmann, the former president of United Theological Seminary, for her unfailing support. Dr. Deichmann provided me with a substantial scholarship when I had despaired and lost hope of continuing my studies. Thanks to Dr. Joni Sancken and Dr. Peter Bellini, UTS faculty members, for their insights. My friend Rosario Picardo at Mosaic is to be credited for playing a double role in my life. Rosario has been my co-pastor for the newly planted Mosaic Church and my mentor overseeing this project. Many thanks as well to my other co-pastor, Wayne Botkin. Rosario and Wayne made this project possible. Together, we share a vision to reach out to international communities. Many thanks to Dr. Vance Ross for his support and encouragement.

A special thanks go to my friend Dr. L.D. Ervin for his valuable advices. Thanks are due to my Arab colleagues at the Arabic Bible study, for their invaluable input and contributions. I am also thankful for my colleagues in the Rooted: Church Renewal and Revitalizing peer group for their encouragement and valuable comments.

This work would not have been possible without library staff, especially for Dr. Sarah Blair's willingness to read my papers and provide valuable comments. Dr. Blair demonstrated her enthusiasm about my writing in many ways, even in a faculty board meeting. I wish to present my special thanks to Erin McKenzie, my editor, who helped shape my writing. Additionally, a long list of friends and colleagues helped through discussion and reading. Thank you also to my best friends and supporters, Nabiel and Nadia Bakhit. In addition, my thanks go to my friends Roger Brucker, who read my manuscript, and Wayne Zwart for his support. For all, I am deeply grateful.

Dedication

This project dedicated to the spirits of my parents—
without their sacrifices, I would not be here—
and to my children, Laura, Andrew, and David

Abbreviations

NASB All Scripture quotations, unless otherwise indicated, are taken from the New American Standard Bible.

LXX The Latin word septuāgintā literally "seventy," often abbreviated as LXX and sometimes called the Greek Old Testament.

ISIS The Arabic name: dāʿish, is a radical Islamic group that claims to be a global Islamic Caliphate.

People fail to get along because they fear each other; they fear each other because they don't know each other; they don't know each other because they have not communicated with each other.
—Dr. Martin Luther King, Jr.

Foreword

I first met Ayad Attia upon his arrival as a student at United Theological Seminary (UTS) in Dayton, Ohio, where I serve on the faculty. At the time, the school was expanding its international program and I was thrilled we had recruited our first student from Egypt. Little did I know what rich experiences and insights he would bring to our learning community!

Already a pastor and leader in Christian education in his Muslim-majority country, Ayad brought with him a depth of understanding from observing, and experiencing personally, the effects of inter-religious conflict. At the same time, he possessed a passion for sharing the gospel of Jesus Christ among the people of his homeland, which had the very real potential for placing him at odds with many of his neighbors and Egyptian authorities.

As a Christian living in the USA, a context of religious freedom with a benevolent appreciation for the Christian faith, I had often wondered what it would be like to live in a place without these benefits. Ayad became my teacher in these matters. Not only did he offer important perspective from his experiences, but his studies in approaches to Christian/Muslim relationships charted a pathway to understanding how a Christian can become a friend, pastor, and sometimes a welcome evangelist among Muslims.

When Ayad began the Doctor of Ministry program at UTS, he invited me to serve as a member of the committee overseeing his academic work, so I have been privileged to learn from his research insights over the past several years. His explorations into biblical, historical, and theological foundations for Christian/Muslim relationships pave the way for new approaches to this ministry, grounded in the love of Christ for all humanity.

This book opens the door to reveal insights from the author's first-hand experiences as a Christian in a Muslim-dominated country. Even more, it unearths valuable findings from Ayad's diligent research into the history and theology of Christian/Muslim relationships. As the reader, you will be challenged to learn from biblical and historical insights in this field. You will be invited to accompany others putting into practice the gospel of the unconditional love of God in Jesus Christ among neighbors coming from a worldview different from your own.

Wendy J. Deichmann
President Emerita and Professor of History and Theology
United Theological Seminary
Dayton, Ohio, USA

Contents

Abstract -- I
Acknowledgement -- II
Dedication -- IV
Abbreviations --- V
Foreword -- VII
Preface -- 1
Introduction --- 8

Chapter One -- 13
    Bridging The Social Gap Betweeen Arab, Christians And Muslims: Why It Matters?

Chapter Two -- 37
    Love Thy Neighbour: The Good Samaritan

Chapter Three -- 68
    Muslims And Christians Interaction: A Historical Model

Chapter Four --- 88
    Neighbor's Love: A Theological Understanding

Chapter Five --- 108
    Cognitive Minority: Can Make A Difference?

Chapter Six -- 128
    Why Arab Christians Stopped Socializing With Their Neighbors? Case Study

Conclusion--162

Appendix
- *A.* Consent To Participate------------------------------------ 164
- *B.* Project Registration---166
- *C.* Research Project Schedule----------------------------------168
- *D.* Questionnaires--170
- *E.* Individual Interviews And Devotionals---------------------181

Bibliography--183

Preface

Martin Luther once said: "I am convinced that men hate each other because they fear each other. They fear each other because they don't know each other, and they don't know each other because they don't communicate with each other, and they don't communicate with each other because they are separated from each other." He also stated, "hate cannot drive out hate only love can do that. Love is the antidote to fear. Perfect love casts out all fear."

Love and fear are mutually exclusive. They cannot stand together. We cannot love and fear someone at the same time. Love produces boldness that casts out fear. Fear is also called unbelief. Jesus asked his fearful disciples, *"Why are you so faithless?"* Fear and faith cannot coexist. Fear is a bad master but could be a good servant. Healthy fear functions positively to make us cautious and gives us the courage to confront our fear openly. Unjustified and unrealistic fear, like anger, bitterness, and anxiety are negative emotions that can lock us in bondage and bring great harm into our lives.

Fear is one of the most crippling things in building relationships with the Other-Different in the Middle East. Fear holds us back from engaging with our neighbors. It separates and keeps us living in a self-made prison of an irrational world.

Recently, I came across the story of the last Japanese soldier who surrendered himself after the end of World War II. He spent almost three decades in the jungle in the Philippines as a captive of fear, refusing to believe that WW II had ended in 1945 with Japan's defeat. The soldier, whose name was Hiro Onoda, has a very interesting story. The last soldier to surrender, Onoda remained in hiding until 1974 when he decided to surrender himself to the Filipino army. While in the jungle with three of his colleagues, he waged a guerrilla war in which he killed 30 Filipino people whom he suspected were Japan's enemies. He waged his own war where there was no war.

In his paranoid hiding, Onoda lost two of his companions and killed 30 innocent people. He had cut himself out of the real world and rejected all rational appeals. He lived in a fantasy world of his own imagination, controlled by fear.

Fear Cuts Us Off from Reality
Let me share my personal story of overcoming fear. I was a parent of a teenage daughter who lives in an anti-Christian faith culture. It has not always been that way but over time things changed. As a parent, I had been overwhelmed by stories of the abduction of Christian girls who were tortured, raped, and forced to convert to Islam. Sometimes they ended up in sex trafficking. I had long battled fear and concern about the safety of my children, especially my daughter.

For many years, I lived with this kind of fear. I became captive to fear. I remember one night when my daughter was in high school, she went out with her friends. She was supposed to come home early but she was late for some reason and her cell phone was off. You can't imagine how much fear I had that night. I was crazy, insane, helpless, and powerless. All my fears rushed out to paralyze me. Later, I realized that I did not even pray.

Later on, out of my fears, I decided to send my daughter away to a safe environment after she finished high school. With the help of a friend, I found her a scholarship in Poland. At the age of 17, I sent my daughter away. The years passed and my daughter settled herself well in Poland. In August 2014, less than two weeks before I came to the States, my daughter flew from Poland to see me before leaving. It happened at the time that I was invited to preach in a rural area two hours away from Cairo. My daughter, her mom, and I were on that trip.

Suddenly, my worst fear fell upon us! We were under mob attack! It was the worst thing in all my life. But God in his mercy used it to transform my life and made me grow.

In Egypt, because Sunday is a working day as it is in all Islamic countries, we have two worship services. The main service is in the evening. We planned to stop in the morning to see my sister, who lives nearby, then go to the church in the evening. After visiting her, we lost our way in a remote village where a little boy fell off his dad's motorcycle against the side of our car.

When I got out of our car to check on the boy, the father attacked me. He was about to stab me with a knife. This radical Muslim noted that my daughter was not wearing head covering, *hijab!* It was obvious that we were Christians. My daughter shouted to me, "Dad he's crazy… Let's go!" We had to get back into the car and drive away. The motorcyclist shouted, "The Christians have killed my son!" This commanded attention and aroused the anger of nearby villagers.

Unfortunately, I had driven onto a dead end road. There was no escape! All the village motorcycles were roaring after us. The violent, angry crowd surrounded our car. They dragged me out of the car, punched me, and kicked me all over my body. One man used a concrete block to strike me on the head. My daughter and her mom were still in the car when the angry villagers started throwing concrete blocks at the car.

The scene was absolute chaos. Some people jumped on the hood and the top of the car. Broken glass was flying everywhere. My daughter and her mother were struck and had numerous bruises on their faces. I was separated from them for half an hour and they did not know if I was still alive or dead. Later, we were taken to the police station. It was clear right away that we were the victims and we suffered harm and the boy was unhurt. We stayed five hours in the police station. Why so long?

In sectarian clashes in Egypt between Muslims and Christians, the government and the police normally do not intervene. It usually ends with Christians being killed or forced to forfeit their homes. When the police do intervene, it is to ensure that Christians have agreed to abandon any legal rights. Muslims will not be condemned.

In our case, the involvement of a pastor or a church would make a sticky political situation that must be contained. Two officers from the National Police Security headquarters, the main domestic security agency of Egypt, were sent to the police station to make sure the incident was contained. In minor accidents, if the two parties reconcile, they can be discharged from the police station. During these five hours the police were trying to convince me to reconcile with my attackers so they could not be blamed. (Remember, this is a culture of honor and shame.) After we were released from the police station, the emergency room doctor made four stitches in my head and treated several bruises on my face and body. My daughter had a black eye. It was a dangerous ordeal, but in it we saw God's hand stretched out to save us from death.

This incident caused my entire family much fear, anxiety, and trauma. We have seen such anti-Christian anger and violence becoming more frequent over the last decades in Egypt. Such hostility makes it hard to love people we call neighbors. The question is, how was I feeling during the attack? Honestly, I was terrified. I was not sure we would survive. I was crying to God while I was fleeing for help. And even though I was beaten and injured, I was not thinking about my own pain. I was thinking about my daughter and her mom.

The fact is that at the beginning of the attack, my daughter was the one who defended me! Later, when I was taken away from the car and beaten, I was less concerned for my life - and more frightened about what was in store for her and her mom.

Adversity can be a catalyst for either personal growth or setback. When we are hurt by somebody, we have the choice: either harbor anger and bitterness or forgive those who have hurt us. The attach I have described above was the most painful experience I ever had. Through the humiliation and the trauma I had been through, God in his grace used that painful moment as a catalyst for personal growth. This devastating accident was used by God to change my life and calling to ministry. This what I call God's providence. God's providence not only saved us from certain death, it also made things work out the benefit of my family, and me.

This Experience Has Taught Us:
1. That to use the gift of God's providence, we have to try to see the whole scene from God's point of view. As a family, we were reunited. Our two boys joined us after the accident, and we went into a quiet place to recover. We struggled to find an answer to the question WHY? Why did we suffer harm and humiliation? It was crystal clear to us that this attack was not personal. We suffered simply because we are Christians. Then we began to see our attackers as victims, victims of ideology and poverty. Ideology makes Christians like us enemies. Thinking that way opened us to find reasons to forgive and release our attackers.

2. To see our attackers being used as tool in Satan's hands. The Bible teaches that our main struggle is not against humans. "For our struggle is not against flesh and blood, but against the rulers, against the authorities, against the powers of this dark world and against the spiritual forces of evil in the heavenly realms." (Eph. 6: 12)

   It was better to see the event as impersonal and release our attackers, than to hold on to resentment. It was also a time when we as a family thanked God for saving our lives.
3. To understand that in releasing my innermost fears, I can be a better neighbor.
4. To recognize that my underlying problem was that in my fear I was afraid to trust God with my life and the lives of the members of my family. Whom do I most trust? God, or myself? I feared allowing the God who runs the universe to run my own business. I had trusted myself more than I trusted God. But I have learned that my real problem was that I wanted to retain control of my world. I let my unrealistic fear drive my life. This taught me to trust God more than I trust myself. I have learned not to let my fear drive my life.

Nelson Mandela once said. "I learned that courage was not the absence of fear, but the triumph over it. The brave man is not he who does not feel afraid, but he who conquers that fear."

I knew that I was set free because when I came to Dayton, Ohio I had to change my dissertation focus from Christian education to inter-faith religion. I am trying to reach out to my Muslim neighbors and build bridges. I make many friends of former adversaries.

I am no longer haunted by what happened to me. No more trauma, no more fear, no more anxiety. Perfect love to my neighbors. Needless to say, I am not trying to argue that I am a hero free of all kinds of fears. I am still vulnerable, like any human, and I will learn to overcome all kinds of fears by love - not as a slave of fear.

As a Middle Eastern Christian minister, out of my experience, I tried to find out why we had to suffer all this pain. Why is there a social gap between Christians and Muslims in Middle Eastern cultures? I tried to explore a biblical, theological, historical, and sociological understanding to help my Christian community build a meaningful relationship with their neighbors. I hope you will find this journey a little help to you as well.

Introduction

Middle Eastern societies have suffered for centuries from mutual misunderstanding, mutual mistrust, and tireless efforts to amalgamate the other into their religion. In a multi-religious society, all efforts have to be made to appreciate diversity and differences, to know the other as the other understands himself/herself. Yet Christians and Muslims share something profound—that is the common love of God and love of one's neighbor. This project will call on Christians and Muslims to put aside dogmatic differences and move toward each other.

Throughout Arab history, fundamentalist tendencies from both Christian and Islamic groups have fostered an air of suspicion and distrust that have prevented these groups from working together. Yet, history also shows that when the two groups chose to work together for the common good, the results were progress and prosperity of their countries. Sociologist and theologian Peter Berger cites how such radicalization creates cognitive minorities rendering them unable to engage the other.

My hypothesis is that when Arab Christians and Muslims are aware that they are a cognitive minority/majority, they will seek to overcome this tendency by being open to cultural challenges and working cooperatively with the other. Three sessions were used to test cognitive minority awareness as a means to overcome the relational divide. Using the qualitative research method, devotions, and individual interviews, the results showed change, though marginal, due to subsequent challenges when returned to their respective communities.

This project was undertaken in the field of inter-religious and intercultural dialogue. However, it is not intended to be an inter-religious dialogue, but rather it is aimed to stimulate, equip, and mobilize Middle Eastern Christians in the USA to overcome their intimidation, complacency, inertia, and be prepared to engage with their neighbors and initiate meaningful social relationships in response to God's love. The interdisciplinary fields of sociology and religion will provide keen insights into research and implementation. The project will utilize a transformative biblical, historical, and theological educational model to help individuals make meaning of his/her experiences through a process of critical self-examination in order to make a change.

This project is comprised of six chapters. The first addresses the author's personal background and ministry journey. The author's early life, education, and the environment in his upbringing in Egypt, followed by his setting in the United States, have demonstrated to him that there is divisiveness and disunity between Christians and followers of Islam. This has manifested in mistrust, fear, and prejudice. The author will describe his intimate involvement in daily life amid religious conflict in his native Egypt. He will seek to discuss his ministerial experiences, the ministry context, and the synergy of both to gain prospects for a future reconciliation between Middle Eastern followers of Christianity and followers of Islam in the greater Dayton, Ohio area. The author believes that his childhood and his ministerial journey and skills as a Protestant pastor—who has experienced God's healing from intimidation and prejudice—have combined to equip him to help in this reconciliation process. To address the topic, the author intends to begin from his own experience as someone born and raised in an Islamic culture as well as from his experience in ministry.

In Chapter Two, the author will examine the biblical concept of treating the stranger who sojourns with the Israelites as the native in the Old Testament context. And "love your neighbor as yourself," in the New Testament context. The parable of the Good Samaritan from Luke 10: 25-37 will exegete within the context of the first century with a look at various missio-logos readings of the parable in general and the interreligious dialogue in particular.

The author will explore Luke 10: 25-37 in-depth as the biblical foundation for the project, asking the following questions. What is Jesus' point of telling the Good Samaritan parable? What is Jesus' definition of the good neighbor? How does Jesus' parable sound to a first-century Middle-Eastern audience? How does it sound to Luke's readers who inferred that the man who felt compassion toward the wounded man was non-Jewish? What kind of hero does the audience expect in the parable of the Good Samaritan? Who, in the end, proved to be a neighbor to the man who fell into the robbers' hands? Is the parable about how the law should be read, interpreted, and therefore obeyed? The project will take a closer look at the historical commentary of the parable and ask the question, "Why was the parable rarely read and interpreted as it was supposed to be—as an interreligious dialogue?"

In Chapter Three, the author will examine the history of the Christian-Muslim interfaith dialogue in a Middle Eastern context to discover an example we can follow. This chapter will address the question, "How is the Christian, who lives in a nation with people of other faith backgrounds, supposed to respond to the Other-different?" The author selects Timothy I the Patriarch of Baghdad (780-823 AD) as a prominent and impressive historical leader of the Eastern Church. By studying Timothy's biography and his apology before Caliph Mahdi, we can learn lessons about how Christians thrived under the rule of the Abbasid Caliphs in the late eighth and early ninth centuries. If the two religions could thrive together then, can we hope to again? Timothy's apology before Mahdi, the Abbasid Caliph, can still inspire us theologically and philosophically today.

The apology took place in an era of Muslim rule in Christian countries. Muslims of the time called Christians *Hetariasts*, or *Associators*, because they thought Christians introduced an associate with God by declaring that Christ is both the Son of God and God. Christians of the time called Muslims heretics and Islam the heresy of the Ishmaelite.[i]

Chapter Four is dedicated to discussing the theological obligation of making ourselves neighbors to every person without exception. The question has to be asked: "How should Christians treat the Other-different?" Wesley's doctrine of prevenient grace and free will be addressed. Additionally, the author discusses the importance of building a relationship of love in reaching out to Muslims.

In Chapter Five, the project gleans insights from the intersection of sociology and religion about how religious minorities perceive themselves and function, as well as about how the majority perceived the religious minorities. The chapter will be dedicated to theoretical foundations, asking, "What prevents Arab Christians (in the minority) from being more connected to their Muslim neighbors (in the majority)?" Or, in other words, "How can the Arab Christians go beyond what has been experienced as marginalized minorities?" The author will look at the theory of a cognitive minority according to sociologist of religion, Peter Berger.

Chapter Six designates a transformative biblical educational study that can help individuals make meaning of their experiences through a process of critical self-examination. The model will include three Bible study sessions, first: "Loving One's Neighbor: An Obligation, Duty or Option," Second: "Minorities Can make Change," and last: "Go and Do Likewise" with pre-and post-assessment questionnaires and interviews. The author recruited a focus group from his contacts born and raised in the Middle Eastern context, most born in Christian families and others converted from Muslim backgrounds. The focus group attended three Bible study classes, and some of them were interviewed individually and completed assessment survey questionnaires. The questions included in the interviews and the assessment survey questionnaires pertain to childhood relationships and interactions with followers of the other religion. Additionally, the author was in contact with his mentors, peer group, professional associates, and faculty members for counseling and insights.

The Expected Results of this Project
1. Create and increase a healthy awareness of the importance of loving our neighbor as an essential and integral part of a sound faith and loving God.
2. Stimulate and mobilize the Middle Eastern Christians in Greater Dayton, Ohio to reach out to their neighbors and develop meaningful social relationships with them.

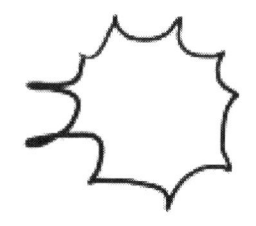

Chapter One

Bridging the Social Gap Between Arab, Christians and Muslims: Why It Matters?

The rise of Islamic fundamentalism in the Middle East in the late 20th century has intensified the relationship between Christians and Muslims, turning a relatively peaceful situation into one of suspicion, animosity, and violence. State wars between Israel and neighboring countries in prior years had reached a stalemate relationship with the exception of the Gaza missile strikes and retaliation by Israel. In the 21st century violence escalated to murder, bombings, and war. A polarized world appears to be the destiny of the immediate future. The religious polarization in the Middle East and elsewhere has manifested as a gap between Middle Eastern communities in the USA as well. This project aims to stimulate, equip, and mobilize Middle Eastern Christians in the USA to overcome their intimidation, complacency, and inertia, and to be prepared to encounter their neighbors and initiate meaningful social relationships as a response to God's love and based on Christ's love.

As a seminary student and resident of Dayton, Ohio, the writer notes that the Dayton area, primarily a Christian community, also has a large community of Christian Arabs and Muslim Arabs. In the opinion of the writer, the Dayton area and the learning environment are ideal to use an educational model and approach to effectively help American Arabic-speaking community in the area to bridge the social gap and reach out to their neighbors. The writer has come to believe that a transformative educational model can help individuals make meaning of their experiences through a process of critical self-examination, which can resolve differences and bring the different groups together under the leadership of God.

Context: Arabic Community in Dayton

In 2014, the United Theological Seminary in Dayton offered the writer a full scholarship to study for a Doctor of Ministry degree. Shortly after arriving in Dayton, he contacted the South Dayton Presbyterian Church. As an Arabic speaker and a Christian among Muslims, he found himself in a unique position here. Some 2,000 Arabic speakers live in Dayton, mostly Muslims. There were 1,100 Arab students at the University of Dayton in 2015. The writer has described being born and raised as a minority in the Middle East, a Christian affected by the Muslim culture. The writer found himself in a reverse situation in the U.S. Here, Arab-American Christians join a supposedly Christian majority in the U.S., while their Muslim counterparts are a minority (often facing discrimination).

The greater Dayton area has a large Arab Christian community, comprised of two churches. One is a Coptic Orthodox Church, located in Miamisburg and affiliated with the Coptic Orthodox Church of Egypt.[1] It is known as the ancient Church of Alexandria. The other

---

[1] Coptic is the traditional name of the Eastern Orthodox Church of Egypt. The Coptic Church belongs to the Oriental Orthodox family, which defines itself by rejecting the Council of Chalcedon canons: namely, Christ has two natures, one human and one divine that are perfectly united in one person. The Coptic distinguishes itself by the principle that Christ has a single nature derived from two

is the Maronite Eastern Catholic Church, affiliated with the Roman Catholic Church.[2] Aside from these two major denominations, there are only a small number of Protestants, especially from Egypt and Lebanon.

Both the Coptic Orthodox Church and the Maronite Catholic Church are traditional churches that believe in baptismal regeneration, as well as in the real presence of the literal body and blood of Christ in the Eucharist.[3] The teaching places weight on baptism as the primary means of salvation, along with meritorious works that include liturgical and sacramental rituals, rather than simply a personal relationship with Jesus Christ. Personal study of the Word of God is not central to the teaching of the ritual churches. The Catholic Church considers Scriptures to be part of the total experience of the Church, co-equal with tradition. As a member of the church, if a person receives the sacrament of baptism, attends Mass on a regular basis, and confesses his or her sins before receiving the Eucharist sacrament, then he or she is a Christian no matter what else he or she has done.

In addition to the Christian Arab community in Dayton, there is a large Muslim Arab community. There are eight Sunni Masjid Islamic centers (Mosques) and one Shiite Islamic center. The Islamic Society of Greater Dayton was founded in 1978. Its first prayer service was conducted in the International Office at the University of Dayton. Since then many masjids have been founded. There are five pillars of Islam that every Muslim should believe and practice: the official profession of faith (the *Shahada*), five daily prayers (*Salat*), alms-giving (*Zakat*), fasting during the month of Ramadan (*Saum*), and a pilgrimage to Mecca (*Hajj*). In reciting the *Shahada*, a person testifies that, "There

---

natures.

[2] The Maronite Church is the largest Catholic church in Lebanon, Syria, and Israel.

[3] Transubstantiation: according to the Roman Catholic and Eastern Orthodox, the substance of the Eucharistic elements at their consecration become the literal body and blood of Christ while keeping only the appearances of bread and wine. *Merriam-Webster.com*, s.v. "Transubstantiation," https://www.merriam-webster.com.

is no God but Allah, and Muhammad is his messenger," in Arabic. This oral statement makes a person Muslim.

There is almost no sacramental system in Islam, no priesthood, and only a very rudimentary prescribed liturgical life.[4] However, the clerics still have a leadership role to play through what is called *Fatwa*[5]. Islam does have an outstanding devotion to prayer, both to formal public worship and to private prayer.[6] There is an old Islamic mysticism movement called Sufism *taṢawwuf* (literally, "to dress in wool," the term derives from a reference to the woolen garment of early Islamic ascetics as a sign of mysticism and poverty.[7]) Sufism, as the *Encyclopedia Britannica* defines it, is:

> Mystical Islamic belief and practice in which Muslims seek to find the truth of divine love and knowledge through direct personal experience of God. It consists of a variety of mystical paths that are designed to ascertain the nature of humanity and of God and to facilitate the experience of the presence of divine love and wisdom in the world.[8]

Like Christianity, Islam claims to have a mission to all nations that is assured of divine favor and eventual success. The Islamic word *Da'wah* is the Arabic term that instructs Muslims to share their faith with non-Muslims and invite them to Islam. It is the equivalent of the Christian word *mission*. From that word is derived the word *Daa'I*, a missionary in Islam.[9]

However, according to *Christianity Today*, 75 percent of Arab-American citizens are Christians. The writer argues that Christian immigration began long ago because, as minorities, it was difficult for Christians to live under Islam. However, since the late 1990s,

---

[4] James Kritzeck, "Islam and Christian Unity." *Worship* 33, no. 8 (August 1959): 477-481.

[5] *fatwā* is an Islamic legal pronouncement, issued by an expert in religious law (mufti) pertaining to a specific issue, usually at the request of an individual or judge to resolve an issue where Islamic jurisprudence (fiqh) is unclear.

[6] Kritzeck, "Islam and Christian Unity."

[7] *Encyclopedia Britannica*, s.v. "Sufism."

[8] Ibid.

[9] *North American Mission Board* (blog), "Apologetics: Popular Islamic Terms,"

immigration has accelerated due to more attention in several Arab nations on their Islamic identity. This renewed nationalism has placed additional pressure on Christians in those countries, therefore leading to far greater numbers of Arab Christians emigrating to the U.S[10] Being citizens of the United States for many years did not help the Arab Christians change their perceptions of Islam and Muslims. The influence of the Islamic culture is present in how Arab Christians perceive the world. The cultural element is more efficient than the religious.

Arabic Bible Study

Not so far from his arrival, the writer was introduced to an Arabic Bible study hosted by a Christian family. The participants originally came from several Middle Eastern countries. However, with Arabic as the common language, the communication among the group is excellent. All members of the group share the experience of immersion in a common Islamic culture. However, not everyone shares the same historical, social, economic, religious, and cultural heritage. The multi-socio-cultural and religious traditional beliefs from which the group members emerged are Coptic, Phoenician, Chaldean, and Assyrian. All originate in Middle Eastern countries, including Egypt, Lebanon, Syria, Jordan, Iraq, and, most recently, Sudan natives were added. Most are immigrants who have been in the U.S. more than two decades, and a few are refugees.

The group can be accurately described as multicultural with traditional religious beliefs melded in an Arab-Christian-Islamic culture, with the impact of American culture. The group meets every other week and the primary purpose is to study the Bible systematically in a fellowship environment. The group consists of twenty to twenty-five people. The median age is fifty to sixty years old.

---

[10] Todd Hertz, "Are Most Arab Americans Christian?" *Christianity Today*, web-only (2003).

There is an Iraqi family in the group who had to flee their homeland due to political unrest and religious discrimination after the ousting of Saddam Hussein's secular regime. The husband and wife hold two Ph.D. degrees from England and held important positions in one of the best Iraqi universities. In 2014, after the Islamic State of Iraq and Syria (ISIS) prevailed in Iraq, they learned that two of their elderly relatives, a brother and sister in-law, had been slaughtered by ISIS militants in their home in Baghdad.[11] Christians living in Islamic countries, especially Iraq and Syria, live under threats of violence, terror, and injustice. It is no wonder that most of the Iraqi Christians who arrived in the U.S. are here because they were forced to leave or flee their countries to escape the terror.

Egyptian Christians understand how much it costs to be a Christian and how terrifying it is to share Christ with your neighbor as a minority. The Islamic culture inflicts fear on the souls of Christians. Those who live in big cities like Cairo are familiar with prejudice, especially during the rule of the Muslim Brotherhood *(al-Ikhwan al-Muslimin)*. After the overthrow of Muhammad Morsi, frenzied Muslim mobs chanting inflammatory, anti-Christian slogans were not uncommon.[12] The violence against Christians in the modern era started in 1970, during the Islamic-oriented regime of El Sadat, and has escalated since Morsi's ousting in July 2013. In August 2013, after the violent dispersal of the Muslim Brotherhood sit-ins in Cairo, it has been reported that at least eighty churches were burned down, as well as dozens of other Christian institutions, and that four were killed.[13] Christians are made to feel every day that they do not belong to the

---

[11] The Islamic State of Iraq and Syria (ISIS); (Arabic name: *dā'ish*). ISIS is a radical Islamic group that claims to be a global Islamic Caliphate. As a caliphate, ISIS claims religious, political and military authority over all Muslims worldwide. Abu Bakr al-Baghdad set himself up as a ruler by order of God and a successor of Prophet Muhammad.

[12] Muhammad Mursi was the first Islamist democratically-elected president (June 2012). On June 30, 2013, Mr. Mursi was deposed by the military.

[13] "Egypt: Mass Attacks on Churches," *Human Rights Watch,* August 21, 2013. www.hrw.org/news.

Islamic countries and should move to Western countries. When the writer speaks to his Bible study members on the phone about another Muslim who shows an interest in Christianity, the person with whom the writer is speaking is cautious and reluctant to talk openly. Despite having been in America more than twenty years and enjoying the benefits of U.S. citizenship, they are still victims of the fear of their homeland's police state tactics. Some who have a successful ministry to Muslims still use aliases out of fear and caution.

The result is that Christians exist as a minority in the Islamic countries while trying to live as full and equal citizens. They face life-threatening danger, radical Islamic terror, opposition from other extremist groups, prejudice, hate crimes, and even injustice from authorities. Immigrants and refugees in the West—whether they left their home countries in search of a safer life and equality, or were forced to flee war—risked their lives. Refugee camps overflow with victims of Islamic extremist groups.[14] However, they still love their native countries and still maintain connections with the families they left behind.

Muslim immigrants and refugees now find themselves a minority in a free country in which the majority are Christians. The Arab American Christians with dual citizenship find themselves in a critical situation with their Muslim neighbors and fellow citizens. One of the current American administration's debated policies is to prioritize Christian immigrants from some Muslim-dominated countries, and to try to prevent by executive order [15]immigration those from some Muslim-majority countries entering the U.S. (it remains to be seen whether the U.S. Constitution and the judiciary will ultimately prevail). Are Arab American Christians willing to stand up with their fellow Muslim citizens and refugees who are in a vulnerable situation, suffering from de facto or informal policies that discriminate against them? And will they choose to be good Samaritans and overcome the

---

[14] The reality is that majority of those refugees are Muslims who fled the religious group violence that acts in the name of Islam.
[15] "Trump's Executive Order: Who Does Travel Ban Affect?" *BBC.com*.

prejudices and hatred they experienced in their countries and extend love and support to those newly arrived?

Observation and Evaluation of the Context

Jesus and the Bible teach us that, as Christians, we should love God and our neighbors. However, as the writer launched his ministry at South Dayton Presbyterian Church, he found that some of the American Arab Community still struggle with the issue of welcoming non-Christian neighbors. In fact, some of the group demonstrated clearly on several occasions that they were prejudiced against Muslims and resisted the idea of reaching out to Muslims. As a reaction to President Trump's executive order to ban Muslims from some Islamic countries entering the U.S.A., someone in the group will openly say, "Trump will kick the Muslims out," or, "Keep them out of America," or, "Go home, Muslims."

This is one illustration of how radical Islam in the Middle East has succeeded in convincing people to trade their tolerance in for hatred. You hear Christians say, "They hate us, so we hate them." We can understand why people pay back hate with hate, but Christians are supposed to be more open to forgiveness. If this cycle of retribution and hatred won't disappear, how can we stop the hating? How can we help the community to overcome its fear of Muslims? We must follow Jesus in loving our neighbors, making every effort to bridge the gap between our communities. To work towards this seems nothing less than pious resistance to evil.

Ministry Journey

The writer grew up in a period of relative peace in Egypt between Muslims and Christians. Yet, he has been attacked by a Muslim mob and experienced government pressure and active opposition by neighbors and close friends.

The writer spent his whole life and ministry in a Muslim-dominated country. He was born and raised in Egypt. Egypt is one of the most devoutly Islamic countries. In Egypt, all daily matters are intertwined with the practice of religion. The cloak of religion is draped over all actions and thoughts, even for individuals who do not practice the five daily prayers. For instance, in the Muslim holy month of Ramadan, every Muslim who has reached puberty is required to observe the fast, not eating from dawn until sunset. Even Christians are expected to eat less publicly during Ramadan. In many Islamic countries, a person—regardless of individual faith—can be fined or jailed for eating in public during daylight hours.

Early Life and Education

In Egypt, the writer attended public schools. Because Egypt is an Islamic state, the education system forces Christian children to memorize and recite the Qur'an as part of the Arabic language curriculum. The history of Egypt is also taught to serve and support Islamic ideology. The pre-Islamic histories—the Christian era of Egypt's history—has been entirely omitted from history textbooks. In the same vein, the rich histories of the great civilizations—the Pharaonic, Phoenician, Babylonian, and Assyrian—have been suppressed. Consequently, Muslim children think that Christianity is a "new thing" in their country. (The same is true in Iraq, Syria, Lebanon, and Palestine.) Children in countries like Libya, Tunisia, Algeria, Morocco, and Yemen do not know that they are descendants of ancient Christians. Likewise, this also gives Christian children the impression that they do not belong in or to their homeland. Such distortions, not to mention hostilities and discriminations directed toward Christian children, are common. Christian youngsters struggle and are confused about why they cannot discuss Christ with their Muslim friends.

Being born in a Christian family, living in this biased and hostile environment, the writer also struggled with many questions, namely, why he should be made to recite the Quranic texts even when he found them so critical of his Christian belief? Why should not

Muslim students recite parts of the Bible as well? Why could he not find any texts from the Bible in his school curriculum? Why is the Egyptian era of Christianity—more than ten centuries—overlooked in the school curricula? The writer was also puzzled by the fact that it was not safe to share his religion with classmates who often attacked his beliefs.

Religious Conflicts and Impact

Christians living in Islamic countries find themselves in deep trouble if they speak openly about their Christian beliefs such as Christ's deity, crucifixion, and resurrection, the Trinity, and the Bible as the Word of God, because these are contrary to Muslim beliefs. While the writer had a decent relationship with some of his peers in school, he ultimately felt that Christians were looked upon as a different people. Unfortunately, it is still true today.

The Christian child living in an Islamic country during the formative years develops a deep understanding that he or she does not belong in society, or, at least, that he or she is not a full citizen. The writer's consciousness was shaped by the fact that state and society are religiously and socially biased against Christians. Even a child's own family, as loving and protective parents, warns children not to question Islam or to even to respond to the questions or criticism that others (children or even teachers) raise against the child's own beliefs.

The 1960s and early '70s were a relatively quiet period in Egypt, free from religious conflict between Muslims and Christians. This peace was mainly a result of the political dynamics of the time. The regime of president Gamal Abdel-Nasser was an Arab nationalist ideology, and was secular. On the one hand, it regarded Islamists as its political rivals. On the other, the Muslim Brotherhood's[16] political

---

[16] The Muslim Brotherhood is an Islamic radical group founded in Egypt by *Hassan al-Banna* in 1928 as an Islamist religious, political, and social movement. The movement was banned during Gamal Abdel Nasser's rule. The Brotherhood came to power through a democratic election in 2012 after the Arab Spring and was ousted by the army in 2013.

objective since its inception in 1929 was to restore the caliphate[17]. *Caliphate* was an exclusive and universal Islamic term describing an Islamic ruler (Caliph) ruling over the Muslim *Umma,* "the whole community of Muslims bound together by ties of religion"[18] where sharia law was enforced.

That contradiction of political interest caused inevitable conflict, which led to a clash between the Brotherhood and Nasser in 1954. In that era as a child, the writer had good Muslim friends with whom he used to study. He does not remember that the religious differences were brought to the surface, as he apparently had learned to be cautious. Perhaps the caution arose because, during the time, Nasser had banished the Muslim Brotherhood and put many behind bars after they attempted to assassinate him in 1954. An additional factor to a peaceful society at that time is that the prominent Muslim families felt privileged to protect Christians as their *dhimmi*s or as second- class citizens.

Middle Eastern Christians for ages were considered second-class citizens by the rank and file. They were referred to as *dhimmis*. The word *Dhimmi* is the transliteration of the Arabic word *Zemmi*, derived from the word *dhimma* or *zimma* which refers to the non-Muslims as people protected by Arab-Muslim conquerors. It implies the dominion of the Arab-Muslim over the non-Muslim. Bigotry dispenses pejoratives often. The Arab-Muslims protect the dhimmis (Christians and Jews,) and, in return a poll tax *(Jizya)* was levied for the protection secured for them. Under the Dhimmitude system non-Muslims were granted the right to practice their religious rituals. However, it implies a process of dehumanization and is considered to be a blunt pejorative. The lenient policy imposes many restrictions on the social status non-Muslims could enjoy. Including the denial of their right to build new churches, temples or synagogues, they:

---

[17] A caliphate is an Islamic state in Arabic: *khilāfa,* means "succession," the noun that derived from the word Caliph which mean a successor to prophet Muhammad.

[18] *English Oxford Living Dictionaries*, s.v. "Umma,"

were prohibited from criticizing the Qur'an, expressing disrespect to the Prophet or to Islam, conducting missionary activity, or having sexual relations with or marrying Muslim women. They were not allowed to make their crosses, wine, and pork conspicuous, or to conduct their funerals in public. Riding horses was prohibited, as was erecting houses taller than those of the Muslims. Dhimmis were required to wear clothes that made them recognizable and were barred from holding certain public positions.[19]

A millet system replaced the Dhimmitude system shortly after the Ottoman Empire prevailed over the Middle East and a large part of Europe.[20] The millet system gave non-Muslims the right to be organized as ethnic groups or religious communities to enjoy internal autonomy.[21] Eventually, the millet system was abolished by the liberal *Tanzimat* issued in 1855 by the reformist Sultan Abdulmejid (1839-1861) in his efforts to adopt the modern European standards.[22]

Aggression against Christians does not only take place in Islamic countries. However, it is so prominent that religious persecution in Middle Eastern countries is de facto, except in the case of Saudi Arabia where it is de facto *and* de jure. It has been said that Muhammad recommended to his companions on his deathbed that, "two religions should not co-exist within the Arabian Peninsula."[23]

---

[19] *Encyclopedia of the Modern Middle East and North Africa*, s.v. "Dhimma."

[20] The term millet is the Turkish the transliteration of the Arabic word *Millah* that occurs in the Quran referring to the religion of the Christians and the Jews (Koran 2:120). It is a pluralistic religious system adopted by the Ottoman Empire to allow each religious group (millah) to organize itself under its authority. Cited from *Encyclopedia of Modern Europe: Europe 1789-1914: Encyclopedia of the Age of Industry and Empire*, s.v. "Millet System."

[21] Tarek Mitri, "Christians-Muslim Relations in the Arab World," in *My Neighbor is Muslim: A Handbook for Reformed Churches,* John Knox Series no. 7 (Genève, Switzerland: John Knox, 1990), 8.

[22] Dennis Basic, *Rights of Minorities in Islam form Dhimmis to Citizens,* ebook, (1-56: HR in Islam-Lecture 6 S.pdf, 2015), http://depts.washington.edu/.

[23] Bat Yeor, *The Decline of Eastern Christianity Under Islam: From Jihad to Dhimmitude: Seventh-Twentieth Century*, eBook, 1st ed. (Madison, NJ: Fairleigh Dickinson University Press, 1996).

While more than one religion has existed within the Arabian Peninsula, Christians have nonetheless struggled in Islam-dominated societies for full and equal citizenship. They have grappled with perceptions and realities of being treated as second-class citizens. The persecution varies from country to country and differs in application in rural and urban areas across the same country.

In 2006 the Barnabas Fund listed ten categories of persecution faced by Christians who live as a religious minority in their countries: societal discrimination, institutional discrimination, employment discrimination, and legal discrimination. The list included harassment such as suppression of Christian missionary activity, suppression of conversion to Christianity and forced conversion from Christianity, suppression of corporate worship, violence against individuals, and community oppression.[24] For instance, many Egyptian Christians complain of employment discrimination based on religion. They are excluded from senior positions either in the military or in the public sector. They cannot hope to become a general intelligence officer, state security police, or president or dean of a university.[25]

In Egypt as in any Muslim-dominated country, construction of new churches is forbidden by statute and would therefore automatically be a huge risk to undertake. Building a new church can be severely punished, not just because it is against the law, but also because it is seen as a direct opposition to the community. However, in certain cases through very complex regulations and good relations with the authorities and the community, new church construction can be permitted by presidential decree. The writer can specifically recall two instances of this. First, in his early childhood, his church required reconstruction. Although the reconstruction proceeded carefully, step-by-step through the bureaucracy, and the church enjoyed good relationships with the people of the village, the writer noticed how the

---

[24] John L. Allen Jr., *The Global War on Christians: Dispatches from The Front Lines of Anti-Christian Persecution,* eBook, 1st ed. (NY: Crown Publishing Group, 2017), 30-33.

[25] Allen Jr., *Global War on Christians.*

people of the church approached the issue with grave concern. The second instance occurred years later when, as a pastor, the writer struggled and prayed for ten years to establish a new church on the outskirts of Alexandria. After navigating all manner of difficulties, the church was finally built where many had lost hope. This story was a classic saga the writer hopes to recount in a book one day. It is a case history of prayer and endurance opposition by following God's strategic guidance.

The writer also vividly remembers boys throwing stones and cursing while the Christian congregation worshipped. It was during a time of tension when the writer began to have many questions again. Why do all these things happen to us as Christians? Why should non-Muslims face inequality in the Islamic states because of their faith? It is not fair! More importantly for a kid asking these questions, why does God allow these bad things to happen to peaceful people? The writer felt that someone should have had an answer for him. However, he could not find answers—even at his local church. To make matters worse, principles were often used in Sunday school and in Christian households to control children in those days. Statements like, "Jesus loves the behaving children," and, "If you misbehave God will send you to hell," were not only contrary to sound Christian doctrine, but also portrayed a God who loves only "perfect" people. It's no wonder that, as a young man, the writer struggled to earn God's love and viewed salvation as something to be earned. Combined, the discrimination against Christians, the writer's unanswered questions, and the absence a true explanation of Christianity left a vacuum in his life until he came to know Christ personally and intimately in 1986 as an adult.

The writer briefly looked at his early educational journey in Egypt in a very quiet era, void of religious violence, as an example of how the consciousness of a non-Muslim child living in an Islam-dominated country develops. In the 1980s and '90s, two waves of jihadist actions occurred as an extension of the Salafist movement.[26] The radical Islamic movement in Egypt was born in the early 1970s. Nasser died in 1970. In the late '70s Egypt witnessed a strict Islamic reformation as a result of the Islamic tide called the Salafist movement, *El Gama'a al Islamiah* (the Islamic Group). The emergence of the radical Islamic Salafist Groups and the return of the Muslim Brotherhood to the scene were encouraged by president Muhammad Anwar el-Sadat.[27] To consolidate his presidential power and to combat the growing number of Nasserites and communists, Sadat encouraged the launch of the Islamic movement in universities[28] Sadat released Muslim Brotherhood leaders from prisons for the same purpose. The movement culminated in Sadat's assassination by his soldiers during the annual victory parade in October 1981.

Like any other Christian child living as a minority in an Islam-dominated country, the writer went from childhood to young manhood with negative stereotypes of Islam and Muslim. These stereotypes have resulted in inherent bias, fear, and hatred.

The Islamic world categorizes all Western countries as Christian. When anyone insults Islam, like the Danish cartoons of the Prophet Muhammad did, such insults are perceived as Christian assaults on Islam. Insults demand violent jihad, such as radical Muslim crackdowns on Middle Eastern Christians. One result is that angry Muslims swell the ranks of militant terrorists. In rural areas the local mosques broadcast urgent calls for jihad against "infidel" Christians and provoke Muslims to take up the sword to defend Islam locally [29].

---

[26] The Salafist is a more radical Islamic group called Sunni Muslims. "All Salafists take a fundamentalist approach to Islam, emulating the Prophet Muhammad and his earliest followers—*al-salaf al-salih*, the "pious forefathers"—right down to their facial hair. They reject religious innovation, or *bida* [heretical doctrine] and support the implementation of sharia (Islamic law)." Cited in *The Economist*, "Salafism: Politics and the puritanical."

[27] Mohamed Anwar al-Sadat was the third president of the Arab Republic of Egypt from 1970-1981. Sadat came to power after Nasser's death in 1970.

[28] Barry Rubin, *Islamic Fundamentalism in Egyptian Politics*, (NY: Palgrave Macmillan, 2002), 6.

[29] Mosques broadcast from loudspeakers mounted on tall minarets. Five

Egyptian Christians were and still are vulnerable to discrimination, prejudice, and violence. Recently, the Islamic State militants were targeting the Copts in Sinai.[30] Thus, hundreds were forced to flee from North Sinai after many were shot, burned alive, or beheaded in their homes.

    Arab Christians are fearful to share the gospel with their neighbors simply because Islamic culture has instilled fear and ill-will. Christians also tend to allow the fear to prevent them from loving their enemies. This context of deep prejudice and discrimination against Middle Eastern Christians, coupled with the package of honor and shame, it may be understandable why a Syrian Christian family would oppose their son's marriage to a former Muslim girl. During a recent pastoral visit, the writer came across one family's secret, kept to themselves for seven years, that illustrates the issue. The issue was that the family's thirty-two-year-old son had fallen in love with an Iranian woman. The family struggled with the idea that their own son would marry a woman who was formerly a Muslim. The parents never even met the woman. She moved to California six years ago. However, the parents discovered that their son was still in contact with this woman, and he refuses to accept any other marriage the family proposes. He is emotionally torn between his girlfriend and his parents. The mother is torn between seeing her son unhappy and the idea of accepting a woman who professed another faith, even though she has left it long ago.

    Wherever fear exists, there can be no love. Fear arises from the unknown, and, in a violent society, from bad experiences. At question here is how to help the community to overcome its fear of Muslims next door, at the grocery, and in each city. Communities are made up of individuals. The individual attitude change must fuel and empower

---

times a day there is the call to prayers and preaching, including at dawn and sometimes as early as 4:00 a.m.

    [30] The word Copt (Qibt) the collective is an Arabic word derived of the Greek word Aigyptos by the Arab rulers of Egypt to coptos.

community transformation. This is the only peaceful way to follow Jesus in loving our neighbors.

Are we fulfilling God's commandment? Do we love our neighbors as ourselves? It is good to know how an outsider sees us. Recently, the writer met an American missionary who had just returned to the States from a mission trip to Egypt. This missionary is interested in helping the native churches in the Middle East reach out to their Muslim neighbors. During a discussion about recent efforts made to reach out to Muslims, he observed, "Yet, Egyptian Christians do not love their Muslim neighbors." Although the statement was painful, it is true. Jesus taught us to love our neighbor. The apostle John said, "There is no fear in love. But perfect love drives out fear." (1 John 4:18).

Overcoming Cultural and Religious Prejudice

Many Christians do not engage in business relationships or friendships with non-Christians because they misunderstood Paul's warning in 2 Cor. 6:14 against binding together with unbelievers. Does Paul's statement mean that any association with unbelievers is forbidden? Most certainly the answer is no. If we look closely at the context, we find Paul warning Christians about two things. First, he warns against being yoked together with unbelievers, which pertains primarily to marriage. Second, he warns against committing idolatry. If Paul forbids Christians to have relationships with non-Christians, how can we understand his statement to the Philippians in 2:15: "shine among [a warped and crooked generation] like stars in the sky." In 1 Cor. 5:10, although Paul advised his Christian readers to avoid the immoral Christian among them, he instructed them that as Christians they are not called to withdraw from the world because of the world's immorality. Jesus prays that God would not take his disciples out of the world, but rather allow them to stay in the world and protect them from the evil one.

Since there is a fundamental contradiction between the Quran and the Jewish-Christian Scripture, Muslims accepted the notion that Jews and Christians altered their scripture. Most of the Muslims the writer has met believe or accept the notion that Jewish and Christian scriptures are corrupted. How can our Muslim neighbors gain better understanding without getting good information from us as Christians? There have been few to no efforts to engage our communities at any level of dialogue on this subject. As Christians and Jesus followers, we must make every effort to reach out to our Muslim neighbors. We ought to strive to impact our community as individuals by building person-to-person or family-to-family relationships. The history of the Muslim-Christian collective interfaith dialogue, at least in the writer's context, has shown a futile endeavor. We should nonetheless take the initiative to build bridges of communication between our community and theirs, and to connect with our Muslim brothers and sisters.

The question as followers of Jesus is how we can love our Muslim neighbors while remaining separate from them. The gulf is encouraged by both faiths as a practical matter. Are our communities mentally, culturally, and spiritually prepared to reach out to them? Are we ready for an interfaith dialogue? Too often dialogue turns to argument based on well-established disagreements.

Jesus teaches us to be the salt of the earth and the light of the world. How does the salt preserve food and makes it tasty? How can we become a light to those individuals who live in darkness? Jesus associated himself with individual publicans, sinners, and tax collectors. According to the Mission Network News, eight out of ten Muslims have never met a Christian, a true Christ follower.[31] If we do not reach out to individuals, how can they know who Christians are? Muslims have many misconceptions about Christians. For example, they believe that there is only one God. Not understanding the Christian Trinity, they believe Christians are infidels who worship three gods. Their individual confusion can turn into great joy and surprise when they

[31] *CBN News*, "Christians and Muslims - How to Bridge the Gap."

find that all Christians believe in one God. Christians and Muslims both believe that the word *God* (or *Yahweh*) is translated in Arabic-language Bibles to the same word that the Quran uses for God, *Allah*. Arabic-speaking Christians still use the word *Allah* to mean *God*. Ultimately, the conversation should not have anything to do with superiority of one belief over another, nor should these conversations focus first and foremost on proselytizing and conversion. Rather, building communities is about obeying God's commandment to love others as we love ourselves.

The writer has a Saudi friend who arrived in the States with many preconceived ideas. He believed that America was a Christian country, that Christians are immoral, and that Christians hate Muslims. His father—for his safety—urged him to use a Christian name instead of his Islamic name, Muhammad. Muhammad's views dramatically changed after he lived with two different Christian host families for three years of his study. In numerous earnest and meaningful religious conversations, this Muslim individual began to speak openly about how sin dominates the rigid and hyper-conservative strain of Islam in his country. Several times, he made comparisons between the good cultural Christian qualities and what he knows and has experienced as a Muslim in his Muslim country. The most important aspect about this friend, although he did not take a step to read the Bible himself, is that he has a hungry spirit to hear the Bible's stories. He went back to his country and considered himself to be an ambassador of American culture and people in his country. This man remains connected to his friends and the families who hosted him. Individual relationship building—one Christian to one Muslim—can work. One at a time.

Jesus teaches us in the Sermon on the Mount not only to love our enemies but to bless and pray for those individuals who persecute us. Having lived many years in an Islamic country, the writer emphatically believes that Muslims are like any other people—the good and the bad, the civil and the uncivil. Categorizing Muslims and labeling them as enemies or persecutors is inhuman and harmful.

Groups can be seen as sub-human; this is much more difficult when individuals are known to us. Labeling Muslims goes against God's commandment in Exodus 20:16: "You shall not bear false witness against your neighbor." Labeling a group of people gives the devil a chance to manipulate our thoughts and drive us to bear false witness against and to hate individual innocent people. Most importantly, it can keep us from doing good witnessing to others as Jesus teaches us to do.

In Jesus' day, there was a fierce historical hatred and long-standing prejudice between the Jews and the Samaritans. The Jews looked down on the Samaritans because of a doubtful ancestry and inadequate theology. In Ezra 4:4-5, the Samaritans were one of the adversaries that opposed rebuilding the temple in Jerusalem.(Nehemiah 4: 2, John 4:21) In this context, it might be easy to understand James' and John's response to the refusal of a Samaritan village to welcome Jesus into their community. "James and John said, 'Lord, do you want us to call down fire from heaven to burn them up?'" Jesus immediately rebuked them, and said, "You do not know what kind of spirit you are of." (Luke 9:54) The Samaritans were believed to be the descendants of the people brought by Assyrians to settle in the Northern Kingdom after they conquered it (2 Kings 17: 24-30). However, the Samaritans claim they were the real descendants of Israel, and the place of true worship should be on Gerizim Mountain, not in Jerusalem. (See the claim of the Samaritan woman in John 4:20)

In Luke 10:25-37, Jesus was aware of the historical animosity between Jews and Samaritans when a lawyer approached him asking, "Who is his neighbor?" To the lawyer's astonishment, Jesus told a parable in a way that shows a Samaritan, not a Jewish priest or a Levite, who has shown mercy to the injured man. The Samaritan was the one who saw, felt compassion, went to the victim, and treated him as a neighbor.

The word *neighbor* in Arabic means the one who lives next door to you. This person may or may not be a relative and could be a

Christian or Muslim. However, the Arabic in many Bible versions translates neighbor as which either means a relative or the individual close to you. In Jesus' parable, the Priest and Levite were supposed to be the neighbor with godly intentions to the injured man. But this was not the case; the Samaritan demonstrated godly actions. Jesus' parable showed that anybody can be a neighbor, not just people living nearby. Jesus admonishes his audience through the parable, focusing on the question, "Who can I be a good neighbor to?" rather than, "Who is his neighbor?" Any person who needs help is a neighbor. At the end of the parable, Jesus asked the lawyer, "Which of these three do you think proved to be a neighbor to the man who fell into the robbers' hands?" (Luke 10: 36) Who is the real neighbor to the man who had been robbed? His answer was, "the one who showed mercy toward him." He could not bring himself to say, "the Samaritan." The Samaritan saw his neighbor as anyone who needs mercy. The Samaritan did not stop to ask himself whether the wounded deserved his help. He felt compassion, he went to him, and he cared for him. Jesus said, "Go and do the same."

On the other hand, there are many Islamic teachings about doing good to neighbors. Quran 4:36 makes a distinction between relatives and neighbors, as well as between people who live near and people who live far away. The Quranic text stresses doing good to your neighbors. If both the Quran and the Bible stress loving and doing good to the neighbor, why we do fail to reach out to each other?

Surviving Personal Attack

In August 2014, two weeks before traveling to the United States, the writer, along with his wife and daughter, were involved in a traffic accident. God spared their lives from certain death after they were attacked by an angry Muslim mob in a remote village in Egypt. The writer's family had lost their way while driving in a village and almost hit a small child. Although it was not their fault, they stopped to make sure the boy was safe. The father of the boy and some local radical Muslims noted that the women in the car were not wearing head coverings. In retaliation, they pushed and struck the writer for several minutes. Then the villagers gathered because rumors spread that a child had been killed in a car accident. The car was destroyed, and the writer had to go to the hospital after spending almost six hours in the police station. The lengthy stay in the police station was because it was evident that the boy was not hurt and the boy's father had invented the rumor.

The police, sympathetic to the Muslim attackers, procrastinated in the application of the law to protect the assailants. In some cases in Egypt, if the two parties of minor accidents reconcile, the case can lawfully be closed. The police's intention was to release the subject without charge. Their solution was to reconcile all parties so that no one would be charged. It wasn't until after the writer's family was released from the police station that the writer finally received first aid. He received four stitches in his head and had several bruises on his face and body. His daughter had a black eye. It was a dangerous moment, but the writer's family saw God's hand stretch out to save them from the threat of death. It was an unexpected sign that justice is one of God's benefits, even in a Muslim-dominated country, and even though they did not receive full legal justice.

Despite the physical, emotional, and psychological traumas suffered during the incident, the family went through lengthy discussions and prayer, eventually arriving at the understanding that the battle is not with these poor fanatic Muslim people who attacked them. The Bible teaches us that our fight is against spiritual powers. This understanding helped them to overcome feelings of anger and bitterness in their hearts, and to identify what happened as spiritual warfare. At this point, they were able to see their attackers from God's view. The writer is grateful to God that he helped them to make a speedy recovery and align themselves with his will. Moreover, he believes that being subject to spiritual attack may be a sign that the evil one takes our work as a serious threat. Being ready to leave to the

States to begin his study, he felt that God might be preparing him for something bigger, not just asylum in another country.

The Synergy

The writer's early life, education, and the environment in his original context in Egypt and then in the United States context identifies that there are dividedness and disunity between Christians and followers of Islam. That dividedness and disunity manifests itself in fear, prejudice, and hate. The writer describes his intimate involvement in daily living amid the religious conflict in his native Egypt. He seeks to study the prospects for a future reconciliation between Middle Eastern followers of Christianity and Islam in the United States. The author's conviction is that his life as a child combined with his ministerial journey and skills as a Protestant pastor who has experienced God's healing from hatred and prejudice, will equip him to bring about further reconciliation through this study.

The writer understands that ill-will against other religions is harmful. He seeks to grow and set himself to be an earnest Christ follower, a good leader, and a better example. The writer intends to study the history of the Christian-Muslim interfaith dialogue, and to examine the biblical and theological concept of treating the stranger who sojourns with the Israelites as the native in the Old Testament context, and "love your neighbor as yourself" in the New Testament context. In other words, the writer will seek to pursue an in-depth understanding of what God intends us to be as Christians, bridging the gap between themselves and their Muslim neighbors by reaching out to them.

The Summary

In focusing on the needs of our Arab community in greater Dayton, the writer believes it is time to prepare his Bible study group to reach out to Muslim neighbors in Dayton, Ohio. How can we transform the complacent culture of American Arab Christians into the biblical culture of love your neighbor? Is education the only need, or are pastoral, and practical studies most impactful? How can we get over the intimidation and the social gap and build lasting relationships?

Attitude can be difficult to change, but experience is key to doing so. Planting a new church has been one important step in this author's own spiritual journey. Through the author's study in the United States, by serving on the board of the newly planted Mosaic Church, and through his role as international pastor, he and others have planned a non-profit organization called House for All Nations Ministries to sponsor and instill a variety of activities that will help the Christian community bridge the gap between themselves and Muslims.

The writer provides background on this religious conflict. He believes that his background in personal relationships with Muslims and the advancement of civil rights law in the United States, hold the key to fostering "love your neighbor as yourself." Will each be able to shed enough cultural baggage and seek relationships above formalism? Let's throw the heavy baggage in the attic and go forth in God's love. The writer's project will be to encourage and reach out to Muslims and sleepy Arabic Christians with the Word of Truth and the Grace of God. Meet the Muslim neighbor. Be A Good Neighbor.

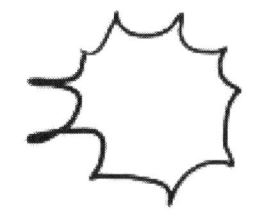

Chapter Two

Love Thy Neighbour: The Good Samaritan

Introduction: Christian-Muslim Relationship

In an open letter entitled "A Common Word Between Us and You," Prince Ghazi bin Muhammad of Jordan, along with many other prominent Muslim leaders, paint a realistic picture of the relationship between Christians and Muslims.[32] He penned it this way: "the Gallup survey showed, we are now actually at the stage where we (both Christians and Muslims) routinely mistrust, disrespect, and dislike each other, if not popularly and actively trash, dehumanize, demonize, despise, and attack each other."[33] This open letter (which, along with a Christian response to the letter, has been published in a book titled *A Common Word: Muslims and Christians on Loving God and Neighbor*) emphasizes that world religious leaders must

---

[32] "The Common Word Between Us and You," an open letter dated October 13, 2007, signed by 138 Muslim leaders from around the world, in response to Pope Benedict XVI's lecture at the University of Regensburg on September 12, 2006. The letter is an attempt to set a common ground for an interfaith dialogue between the two big religions in the world.

[33] "The Common Word Between Us and You."

earnestly work together to resolve the current crisis. Bin Muhammad argues that all must live and let live in order to love thy neighbor. He maintains that his idea of love thy neighbor must be expressed from within our religious scriptures, and must then be applied everywhere.[34]

The two Islamic testimonies that there is no God but *Allah* and Muhammad, his messenger, are the *sine qua* to be a real Muslim. Every Muslim believes that Muhammad is the "seal of the prophets," and reveres the Qur'an as the sacred word of God.[4] These Muslim beliefs do not find common ground with orthodox Christianity, simply because Christian's scriptures do not speak about it. In the same vein, the testimony that Jesus is Lord, and the acknowledgment of his redemption work, his death on the cross and resurrection, is central to the orthodox Christian faith. However, it is considered committing *shirk*, polytheism, or associating someone else with God, according to the Islamic theology. The same is true with the doctrine of Trinity. These are just a few examples of many profound differences between the two faiths.

Middle Eastern societies have suffered for centuries from a mutual misunderstanding, a mutual mistrust, and tireless efforts of amalgamating the other into their religion. In a multi-religious society, all efforts have to be made to appreciate the diversity and differences, to know the other as the other understands himself/herself. The author claims that he rarely finds a Muslim who concedes Christianity as Christians understand it. Similarly, he rarely finds a Christian who perceives Islam as it is understood by a Muslim. Yet there is something profound Christians and Muslims share—that is the common love of God and love of one's neighbor. Christians are to "'Love the Lord your God with all your heart and with all your soul and with all your

---

[34] Miroslav Volf, Ghazi bin Muhammad, Mellisa Yarrington, edt. *A Common Word: Muslims and Christians on Loving God and Neighbor,* (Grand Rapids: MI, Wm. B. Eerdmans Publishing, 2010), 7.

[4] Volf, Bin Muhammad, and Yarrington, edt. *A Common Word: Muslims and Christians on Loving God and Neighbor.*

mind'; and 'Love your neighbor as yourself.' (Luke 10:27) Christians are to love their neighbors even when their neighbors treat them with enmity. This project calls on Christians to know Muslims as they present themselves, and Muslims to understand Christians as they present themselves, as well as shared work on social matters and problems of common concern.

Christians understand that this love of neighbors is a response to God's love for his creation. In the Holy Qur'an, God the Most High admonishes Muslims to enjoin the People of the Scripture—Christians and Jews—into a common word: "'O People of the Scripture, come to a word that is equitable [other translation Common Word] between us and you…' (Al-Imran; 64) The Common Word is a call to set aside the dogmatic differences and live together in peace and justice, with open hearts, minds, and hands. The purpose of this project is to consider how to overcome the religious bigotry, prejudice, and discrimination of Christian-Muslim relationships in the context of a Middle Eastern community. The author examines the parable of the Good Samaritan as an essential biblical foundation for this project. The parable of the Good Samaritan is Jesus' offer to the halachic discussions of the understanding of the commandment to love the neighbor in the first-century Jewish culture.[7]

The Historical Context for the Good Samaritan Parable

The parable of the Good Samaritan is the perfect historical context as a biblical study case; the Samaritans were despised and hated by the Jews and vice versa. For many centuries the Jews looked upon the Samaritans as being more like the Gentiles than like the Jews. The Samaritans were believed to be the descendants of the people brought by Assyrians to settle in the Northern Kingdom after they conquered it. 2 Kings 17:24-30 However, the Samaritans claimed that they were the

---

[7] Richard Bauckham, "The Scrupulous Priest and the Good Samaritan: Jesus' Parabolic Interpretation of the Law of Moses1," *New Testament Studies*, Volume 44, no. 4; October, 1998, 475-489, 476.

real descendants of Israel, and that the place of true worship should be on Gerizim Mountain instead of Jerusalem. (John 4:20.)

Bernard Brandon Scott observes that, "the enmity between the Jew and Samaritan was proverbial. Ben Sirach illustrates the enmity as he writes 'he that eats the bread of the Samaritan is like to one what eats the flesh of swine.'"[10] And also "Two nations my soul detests, and the third is not even a people: Those who live in *Seir*, and the Philistines, and the foolish people that live in *Shechem*. Sirach 50:25–26 The word *Samaritan* is the accusation that Jesus' opponent brings against him of being a Samaritan λέγομεν, possessed with a devil. The enmity reached its highest point in the first century, six to nine CE, when a Samaritan desecrated the temple with human bones during the Jewish Passover celebration.[12]

Samaritans in Luke's Gospel

Luke locates the parable of the Good Samaritan in a major section: Jesus' journey to Jerusalem, which begins in 9:51 and ends at 19:28.[13] This section starts with a negative portrayal of a Samaritan village that did not receive Jesus 9:51-56. In v. 52 Jesus sent messengers ahead into a Samaritan village to prepare for him. The Samaritan people would not receive him because he was on his way to Jerusalem. This illustrates that the general attitude between the Jews and the Samaritans was one of hostility.[14] We also see James' and John's harsh desire to retaliate for the village's insult.

Jesus taught his audience in the Sermon on the Mount that one should not stop at loving one's neighbor, but should extend this to

---

[10] Bernard Brandon Scott, *Hear Then the Parable: A Commentary on the Parables of Jesus,* (Minneapolis, MN: Fortress Press, 1989), 197.

[12] John R. Donahue S.J, "Who Is My Enemy? The Parable of the Good Samaritan and the Love of Enemy," *The Love of Enemy and Nonretaliation in the New Testament,* Willard M. Stewartley, ed. 1st ed., 137–156. Studies in Peace and Scripture. (Louisville, KY: Westminster/John Knox Press, 1992), 141.

[13] Donahue, "Who Is My Enemy?" 137.

[14] Ralph W. Harris, Stanley M Horton, and Gayle Garrity Seaver, *The New Testament Study Bible: Luke,* (Springfield, MO: Complete Biblical Library, 1991), 309.

include one's enemy as well. In Luke 9:51-56 Jesus set an example for his disciples about how to practice tolerance. He refused to seek revenge. Jesus' disciples should not respond to the opposition. "Christians are to be patiently tolerant and magnanimous under provocation. They must be prepared to accept hostility without retaliation or desire for revenge."[15] Paul teaches us that Christians are not to take revenge; they have to leave room for God's wrath. (Romans 12:19) Retaliation has no place in the Christian life.

Luke later conveys two stories portraying two notable Samaritans. The first is in the parable of 10:25-37, in which Jesus surprises his audience in a story about a wounded traveler. Neither a priest nor a Levite proves to be a good neighbor to the injured Jewish man. Only the Samaritan in Jesus' parable kept the law. The other example is in 17:11-19. Out of ten lepers cleansed of their leprosy, only one, a Samaritan, turns back to glorify God and give thanks to Jesus. The other nine were Jewish. Only the Samaritan deserved Jesus' praise: "… your faith has made you whole." (Luke 17:19 KJV)

Luke 9:51-56 tackles the question of how Jesus' disciples should handle others' hostility. Jesus accepts the opposition quietly and refuses to seek vengeance.[18] He rejects the spirit of Elijah. He immediately rebuked them ἐπετίμησεν, "a term often used when Jesus rebukes demons or hostile powers,"[19] and said, "You do not know what kind of spirit you are of." This story shows the Samaritans' hostility toward Jesus and the spirit with which Jesus receives that kind of insult. He refused to seek vengeance on those who opposed him. Jesus' call to love one's neighbor extends to include all ethnic, religious, and racial groups.

---

[15] William R. Farmer, ed. et al. *The International Bible Commentary: A Catholic and Ecumenical Commentary for the Twenty-First Century*, (Collegeville, MN: Liturgical Press, 1998), 1405.

[18] I. Howard Marshall, *The Gospel of Luke (The New International Greek Testament Commentary)*, (Exeter, England: Paternoster Press, 1978), 403.

[19] Donahue, "Who Is My Enemy?" 137.

In this chapter I will argue that hospitable engagement with the other was important to Jesus' teaching, using the Parable of the Good Samaritan as an example. After reviewing the historical context for the parable and the portrayal of Samaritans in the Gospel of Luke, the chapter will look at the literature of the parable and offer insight on whether the parable classified similitude, parable, or exemplary story as well as the patristic Allegorical-Christological interpretation of the parable. Then will look exegetically to the biblical text word by word with its critical analysis. Will conclude by having a look at the parable as an interreligious exchange. Accepting that Jesus calls Christians to engagement with religious others has the potential to transform interfaith relationships.

The Parable of the Good Samaritan

The Literary

The classification of the parable of the Good Samaritan is a matter of debate among New Testament scholars. The dispute is whether the parable classified similitude, parable, or exemplary story.[20] The German scholar, Adolf Jülicher places the parable among four other Lucan parables as an "example story." He asserts that the parable of the Good Samaritan explicitly concluding with, "Go and do likewise" indicates that the parable presents an example to be imitated."[21]

Rudolf Karl Bultmann, conversely, differentiates between the example story and the parable, contending that the element of metaphor is missing from the former. He categorizes the parable of the Good Samaritan with the Rich Fool, the Rich Man and Lazarus, and

---

[20] L. W Mazamisa, *Beatific Comradeship: An Exegetical-Hermeneutical Study On Lk 10: 25-37,* (Kampen: J. H. Kok, 1987), 87.
[21] Klyne R. Snodgrass, *Stories with Intent: A Comprehensive Guide to the Parables of Jesus,* (Grand Rapids, MI: Eerdmans, 2008), 350.

the Pharisee and the Tax Collector, among the Synoptic example stories within a special Lucan material.[22]

Klyne R. Snodgrass argues that labeling the parable of the Good Samaritan as an example story is inadequate and inappropriate. He classifies it, along with four other Lucan parables, as a single, indirect narrative. Snodgrass argues that these five parables "address the reader indirectly by telling of another person, but directly by using the subject that is of concern." He continues, "the Good Samaritan addresses the lawyer and the reader indirectly through the travelers, but the subject is the issue at hand, the love command and the definition of neighbor."[25] He states that "the parable of the Good Samaritan is a single indirect parable, but it comes very close to being a juridical parable. Jesus' concluding question to the scribe requires an answer that is self-condemning."[26]

Snodgrass observes that some New Testament scholars (himself included) see the parable as a metaphor for the reversal of values that the Kingdom brings.[27] Robert C. Tannehill disagrees that it is a reverse value. He states: "the Samaritan does not reverse his situation, but he upsets the expectations of a Jewish audience. He surprisingly fills the role of the one who knows the meaning of the command to love the neighbor."[28]

Llewellyn Welile Mazamisa argues that the parable and similitude are types of analogy or simile. As a comparison between different things, he sees the example story as an illustration of a general principal. He maintains, "if the purpose of this particular parable was to invite a Jewish audience to imitate the model of neighborly concern represented in the leading figure in the story, for such a purpose it

---

[22] John P. Meier, *A Marginal Jew: Rethinking the Historical Jesus,* (Yale University Press, 2016), 62.
[25] Snodgrass, *Stories with Intent*, 352.
[26] Ibid, 13.
[27] Ibid, 348.
[28] Robert C. Tannehill, *The Narrative of Luke-Acts: A Literary Interpretation, Volume 1 the Gospel According to Luke,* (Philadelphia, PA: Fortress Press, 1986), 110.

would have been far better to have made the wounded man Samaritan and the helper a Jewish man outside clerical circles."[29]

Gerhardsson rejects the assertion that the Good Samaritan is an example story, maintaining that the parable is more than a reflection on love of one's neighbor in action. He accepts the idea that the Good Samaritan is a figurative story. For him "the wounded man is Israel. The priest and the Levite are the unfaithful shepherds; the Samaritan is the true shepherd of Israel." [30] According to Thiselton, Gerhardsson sees that "the essence of the parable is not the true neighbor but the true shepherd. In Hebrew the words of neighbor and shepherd look alike (*'rea'* and ro'e'), it is impossible, therefore, that Jesus referred to both neighbor and shepherd."[31] Gerhardsson argues that Jesus draws not only upon the Old Testament imagery of the parable of the Good Samaritan, but that he also makes use of the well-known rabbinic techniques of interpretations.[32]

The Allegorical and Allegorical-Christological Interpretation of the Parable

The patristic biblical interpretation of the parables, in general, and the Good Samaritan, in particular, tended to be allegorical. Scholars Origen and Irenaeus acknowledged an allegorical interpretation of the parable.[33] Augustine later developed further details. He identifies the traveler who fell into the robber's hands, stripped of clothing, beaten, and left half dead alongside the road as representing Adam or fallen humanity. Jerusalem represents heaven or the Garden of Eden. Jericho represents mortality. The robbers

---

[29] Mazamisa, *Beatific Comradeship*, 88.
[30] Thiselton, "Parables as language-event," 437...
[31] Ibid, 438.
[32] Robert W. Funk, *Language, Hermeneutic, and Word of God: The Problem of Language in the New Testament and Contemporary Theology*, (New York, NY: Harper& Row, Publishers, 1966) 203.
[33] Patrick M. Clark, "Reversing the Ethical Perspective: What the Allegorical Interpretation of the Good Samaritan Parable Can Still Teach Us," *Theology Today* 71, no. 3: 300-309.

represent Satan and his angels.[34] The travelers—the priest and the Levite—symbolizing the ineffectual dispensations of the Old Testament; (the law and prophets.) Finally, the Samaritan represents Jesus Christ.[35]

Kenneth Bailey rejects the allegorical interpretation. He states: "with the allegorical method anyone could read almost anything into almost any parable."[36] C.H. Dodd's definition of the parable is "a metaphor or simile drawn from nature or a common life, arresting the hearer by its vividness or strangeness, and leaving the mind in sufficient doubt about its precise application to tease it into active thought."[37] Mazamisa cites Longenecker's observation on the employment of the parables in Jewish and rabbinic literature by prophets and wise women and men as such: "the Jewish interpreters considered the purpose of all biblical interpretation to be the translating into life of the instruction of God—that is, to make the words of God meaningful and relevant to the people in their present situation."[38]

The Lawyer's first question to Jesus: "Teacher: what shall I do to inherit eternal life?" The question regarding inheriting the eternal life is Luke's specifically. It was asked again in Luke 18:18, this time by the rich young ruler: "Teacher, what shall I do to inherit eternal life?" Marshall states that "There is nothing surprising in the question being asked on more than one occasion, since it was a rabbinic theme. Rabbi Eliezer (c. AD 90) was asked by his pupils, "Rabbai, teach us the ways of life so that by them we may attain to the life of the future world."[39]

Luke's specific about the Good Samaritan parable (10: 25-37) according to L. W Mazamisa, is that "The parable is not presented in

---

[34] Ibid, 304.

[35] Ibid, 301.

[36] Kenneth Bailey, *Through Peasant Eyes: More Lucan Parables, Their Culture and style*, (Grand Rapids, MI: Eerdmans, 1980), xxi.

[37] Geoffrey W. Bromiley, ed. *The International Standard Bible Encyclopedia*, Revised ed. Volume 4, (Grand Rapids, MI: Eerdmans Publishing, 1988), 657.

[38] Mazamisa, *Beatific Comradeship*, 88.

[39] Marshall, *The Gospel of Luke*, 442.

the language of the sacred or the language of myth; it is presented in the language of human history, of the profane, that of open drama."[40] He argues that what Jesus portrays in the parable is a skandalon. The Samaritan represents profanity, the outcast, and the despised in the Jewish milieu, the furthest and least expected one of the three passers-by to fulfill the law. The one who, for the Jewish audience, is at the bottom of the religious and moral hierarchy is the one who "came upon him; and when he saw him, he felt compassion." He was the one who showed mercy to a half-dead man in the ditch.[41] Whereas, the priest and Levite, who are on top of the religious and moral hierarchy, acted inhumanely.

The Dialogue Between the Lawyer and Jesus (Luke 10:25-29)

Luke locates the parable in the context of Jesus' journey to Jerusalem. That dialogue (vv. 25-28) parallels partially with the series of theological controversies that Mark and Matthew record during Jesus' last days of ministry in Jerusalem (Mark 12: 28-34; Matthew 22: 34-40).[42] In Matthew and Mark, the question concerns the greatest commandment, whereas Luke's lawyer's question is about eternal life. In Luke, Jesus prods the lawyer to answer his own question.[43] In both Mark and Matthew gospels, Jesus answers the question. However, many commentators argue that the original parable of the Good Samaritan is in verses 30-37a, and Luke has carefully woven the story by linking it with the dialogue between Jesus and the lawyer (vv. 25-28).[44] Luke employs the lawyer's second question: Who is my neighbor? (v. 29) as a connector between the conversation and the parable. As well as Jesus' final admonition in 37b 'Go, an do likewise.'[45] In the

---

[40] Mazamisa, *Beatific Comradeship*, 85.
[41] Ibid.
[42] Daniel Patte, ed. *Global Bible Commentary: Luke,* (Nashville, TN: Abingdon Press, 2004), 149.
[43] Patte, ed., *Global Bible Commentary,* 149.
[44] Ibid.
[45] John Dominic Crossan, *In Parables: The Challenge of the Historical Jesus,* (New York, NY: Harper & Row Publisher, 1973), 58.

scholar's opinion this is to make the parable an example story of a helpful Samaritan.[46]

John Dominic Crossan states that the thesis is that the Good Samaritan as an example story appears unassailable when the story is read with its present overture of Luke 25-29 and its present culminating admonition in 10:37b, 'Go, and do likewise.' He argues that both are "not original and therefore cannot be used to interpret the meaning of the parable of Jesus. Crossan divides the complex 10:25-37 into four layers: the first, the lawyer's question concerning the eternal life in 10:25-28; the second, the question regarding one's neighbor in 10:29; the third, the parable in 30-35; the conclusion in 10:36; the answer in 10:37a; and finally, Jesus' admonition.[49] Most critics consider 25-29 and 37b artificial, not belonging to the parable itself, suggesting that it was added by Luke or was pre-Lucan.[50]

Craig L. Blomberg also notes that "Cadoux rejected the authenticity of all of the brief conclusions or applications most of the parables end, stressing that 'the speaker who needs to interpret his parables is not master of his method.'"[51] Colin M. Ambrose disagrees with that view. He comments:

> This problem is only exacerbated by form-criticism. Recognizing the similarity of 10:25-28 with Mark 12:28-31 and Matthew 22:34-40, it is commonly held that 10:25-28 is material reworked either from Mark and/or Q to create a narrative context for an earlier authentic parable of Jesus. Successfully removing 10:25-28 from the parable legitimates the consensus interpretation of δικαιόω. Yet it may still be asked, even if one understands Luke 10:25-28 as standing alone and not informing the subsequent parable, why did the redactor, whether it is Luke or pre-Lukan,

---

[46] Patte, ed., *Global Bible Commentary*, 149.
[49] Crossan, *In Parables*, 58.
[50] Geoffrey W. Bromiley, ed. *The International Standard Bible Encyclopedia*, Revised ed. Volume 4, (Grand Rapids, MI: Eerdmans Publishing, 1988), 657.
[51] Craig L. Blomberg, *Interpreting the Parables*, ebook, (Downers Grove, IL: Intervarsity Press, 2012), 38.

change the initial question from "Which commandment is the first of all?" (Mark 12:28; cf. "Which is the greatest commandment?" [Matt 22:36]) to "What must I do to inherit eternal life?" If one believes that 10:25-28 is derived from Mark or Q, the substantial redaction of the material points to the author's intent to inform the narrative context of 10:25-37.[52]

However, Blomberg suggests, "it is better to take verses 25-28 as originally belonging with the parable that follows."[53] Likewise, Marshall also argues that, in section 25-29, the theological dialogue works as a direct context of the parable. He maintains it is difficult to imagine the parable without this present setting.[54]

The Exposition of the Text (Luke 10: 25-29)

In verse 25: Νομικός: *Nomikos* is one well-versed in the Law of Moses, a lawyer, a person who is a specialist in interpreting the law of Moses (Luke 11:52), also known as scribe. ἀνέστη: stood up, a social courtesy, a student has to stand up when addressing his teacher as a sign of respect. ἐκπειράζων: to test thoroughly, tempt, make trial of. He shows a cultural respect, but out of an inner corrupt heart.[57] However the word πειράζω can be used on a positive tests like in: Mt 4:11; Lk 22:28; 1 Cor 10:13; Js 1:12. Διδάσκαλε: it occurs thirty-one times translated as a teacher, master, the original word διδάσκαλος, a teacher or an instructor.

The lawyer addresses Jesus as acknowledged for his mastery in his field of learning; he is a Bible teacher, competent in theology.[58] He shows respect to Jesus as a teacher, but the question "was not an

---

[52] Colin M. Ambrose, "Desiring to Be Justified: An Examination of the Parable of the Good Samaritan in Luke 10:25-37," *Sewanee Theological Review* 54, no. 1: 17-28.

[53] Blomberg, *Interpreting the Parables*, 297.

[54] Marshall, *The Gospel of Luke*, 440.

[57] Bailey, *Through Peasant Eyes*, 35.

[58] All the Greek words quotes from Strong's, 1320, http://biblehub.com/greek/1320.htm.

honest one. He wanted to test Jesus' theology while justifying himself."[59] The word κληρονομήσω: means to inherit, obtain (possess) by inheritance, acquire. ζωὴν αἰώνιον (eternal life) "the thought is primarily of life with God after death."[60] Strong's concordance suggests that the translation of the word Κληρονομήσω 'to inherit,' stronger than 'to obtain,' the idea of being qualified now to receive the future blessings from God.

The lawyer's question gives an insight into the theological thought of the day, which was contrary to Jesus' teaching. The thought was that "the eternal life could be earned by performing some heroic act or great sacrifice, once for all."[62] Bailey observes that the lawyer's question is pointless since nothing can be done to inherit something. Inheritance is a legal term that is acquired by descent. He maintains that, in the case of Israel, inheriting the promise land was a gift from God.[63]

Verse 26: Jesus responds to the lawyer's question with a counter-question, "What is written in the Law? How does it read to you?" the word γέγραπται, means it is written or it stands written (in the scriptures), Marshall cites Grundmann's observation that "Jesus is interested in the written law, not the oral tradition." πῶς ἀναγινώσκεις, translated how does it read to you? (NASB) Marshall argues that the question reflects the Jewish method of argumentation. He maintains that the question might be understood by the lawyer as, "How do you recite?" In other words, Jesus directed the lawyer to the way he recited the law "as a part of his regular worship and therefore the lawyer is forced to reply with the words of "Shema." Marshall observes that, by his response, Jesus shifted the theme from "the teaching of Jesus himself to the how the lawyer understands the law, and it is his view

---

[59] Harris, Horton, and Seaver, *The New Testament Study Bible*, 331.
[60] Marshall, *The Gospel of Luke*, 440.
[62] Harris, Horton, and Seaver, *The New Testament Study Bible*, 333.
[63] Bailey, *Through Peasant Eyes*, 35.

which is tested by Jesus."⁶⁶ Instead of testing Jesus he finds himself being tested.

In verse 27: the lawyer answered, "you shall love the Lord your God with all your heart, and with all your soul, and with all your strength, and with all your mind, and love your neighbor as yourself." ἐν ὅλῃ καρδίας with all your heart. The heart is the center of the intellect in ancient Hebrew.⁶⁷ Marshall observes that the list of the phrases in the three synoptic gospels is different from that in LXX. Luke adds διανοίᾳ, mind, at the end of the list. Marshall argues that Luke's wording is distinct from an independent source, that of Mark and LXX.⁶⁸ By citing the mix of part of Shema in Deuteronomy 6:5 and Leviticus 19:18, the lawyer connected the eternal life with loving God and neighbor.

This was Jesus' Matthew answer to an expert in law's question: "Teacher, which is the greatest commandment in the Law? (Matthew 22: 36-39) Bailey states that it is through a love of God that the believer is to approach people. Jesus said, the entire law and all the demands of the prophets are based on these two commandments.

In verse 28: the word Ὀρθῶς, means rightly, correctly, Jesus commends the lawyer for his correct answer. He praises him for his good knowledge and faithful recitation. Jesus recommends him ποίει, to make, practice, *do this*, to put love in practice; to God, neighbor, and you, ζήσῃ, shall live, life (physical and spiritual.) Life is derived—i.e. it always (only) comes—from and is sustained by God's self-existent life. Bailey observes that "the man has the right theology, but the question is, Is he willing to act on it?"⁷³

Verse 29: δικαιῶσαι the original word δικαιόω, has passive meaning: to justify, approved, especially in a legal, to declare guiltless one accused or who may be accused, acquitted of a charge or reproach, declare righteous especially with God. Πλησίον, near, close by; (n.)

---

⁶⁶ Marshall, *The Gospel of Luke*, 442.
⁶⁷ Bailey, *Through Peasant Eyes*, 38.
⁶⁸ Marshall, *The Gospel of Luke*, 443
⁷³ Bailey, *Through Peasant Eyes*, 38.

neighbor; can function as an improper prep., nearby, Jn. 4:5; Πλησίον. Strong's definition could be translated as a friend: Matthew 5:43, any other person, where two are concerned the other (thy fellow-man, thy neighbor). According to the NT, any other man irrespective of race or religion with whom we live or whom we chance to meet (Luke 10:25-37). According to the OT, רֵעַ, neighbor ray'-ah, friend, companion, fellow, a member of the Hebrew race and commonwealth.

The lawyer desires to justify himself by soliciting Jesus' interpretation of who is one's neighbor in the commandments. Marshall observes that the lawyer found himself looking rather foolish after being forced to answer the question he has raised.[78] Who is my neighbor? At Jesus' time, the Pharisees, scribes, and the experts of the law observed detailed rules and traditions that served as a hedge around the commandments (Matthew 23: 4) Therefore the neighbor can be defined according to its position in or out of this circle. Jesus responds with "the parable and a counter-challenge that reaffirms the lawyer's question from one of social identity to one of needs-based mercy."[79]

In her book, *Luke (Westminster Bible Companions)*, Sharon Ringe noted that Luke implies that the lawyer sought a definition for the question, "Who is my neighbor?" He was wondering, "Whom should I love as I love myself?" According to Ringe, "Luke implies that [the lawyer] was seeking a definition of neighbor that would set clear limits about who was to be loved as he loved himself."[80] She continues,

> Does the term include only family? More distant relations? People with whom he shares particular social connections? People within a specific geographical area? The question fits not only a personal concern of someone trying to live a religious

---

[78] Marshall, *The Gospel of Luke*, 447.
[79] John A. Szukalski, *Tormented in Hades: The Rich Man and Lazarus (Luke 16: 19-31 and Other Lucan Parables for persuading the Rich to Repentance,* (Eugene, OR: Wipf and Stock Publisher, 2013), 102.
[80] Sharon H. Ringe, *Luke*, in Westminster Biblical Companion, ed. Patrick D. Miller and David L. Bartlett, (Louisville, KY: Westminster John Knox, 1995), 157.

life, but also the context of Luke's church with its expanding ethnic and geographical boundaries. Just how far does our responsibility extend? By way of an answer, Luke presents a parable.[81]

The parable is Jesus' answer about whom the lawyer should love.

The Exposition of the Text (Luke 10:30-35)

Verse 30: ἀνθρωπος: means a man, human, mankind a man. The parable presupposes that a Samaritan passerby found an injured Jew lying on the roadside. Bailey observes that a first-century Jewish audience would naturally assume that the traveler is a Jew.[82] Marshall states that the story intentionally leaves the man without description; he can be any man. Κατέβαινεν: means to go down, descending, the road between Jerusalem—2,500 feet above sea level—and Jericho—800 feet below sea level—the road steep through the desert of 3,300 feet over seventeen miles.[84] The road is narrow and winding in a barren desert, with caves that provide shelter to thieves.[85] The road gained a bad reputation throughout history as "the path of blood." Josephus describes it as wild and barren.[86] Travel was considered risky and unsafe to anyone traveling alone. The word λησταῖς, a robber, a bandit, "is a thief who also plunders and pillages–an unscrupulous marauder, exploiting the vulnerable without hesitating to use violence." Περιέπεσεν, fall into the midst, totally surrounded by.

The word ἐκδύσαντες, means to strip one of his person or garment or both. They stripped the traveler of his identity. Bailey argues that the first-century "Middle Eastern world was and is made up of various ethnic-religious communities." He maintains that the traveler is able to identify strangers two ways; by his speech and by his manner of dress. The word ἀφέντες either mean to send away or leave

---

[81] Ringe, *Luke*, 157.
[82] Baily, *Through Peasant Eyes*, 45.
[84] Marshall, *The Gospel of Luke*, 447.
[85] Baily, *Through Peasant Eyes*, 45.
[86] Scott, *Hear Then the Parable*, 194.

alone, permit or leave him ἡμιθανῆ, half-dead. Bailey recounts stories of people who had been victims, beaten, stripped, and left naked by the band of robbers who ambushed travelers on the side of the road. Being stripped of his identity and beaten, the traveler became an anonymous person, "reduced to a mere human being in need. He belonged to no man's ethnic or religious community."[92]

An anonymous man throughout a story to a Jewish audience would be naturally assumed to be Jewish. The position of the audience is critical, as Scott observes; in Jesus' parable the hearer is Jewish and sees the victim as also Jewish, and Luke's implied reader is Gentile. Henceforth, the hearer is prepared and await a hero's arrival.[94]

Verse 31: The word, υγκυρίαν, means coincidence, the original word, συγκυρία is used only in Lk 10:31. It means a coincidence, accident, chance, "to happen co-incidentally." Strong's concordance observes that any coincidence or chance, properly, was "God's providential arrangement of circumstances – all achieving his eternal purpose in each scene of life." Thence, the verse would be understood this way; According to [divine] co-incidence συγκυρία a certain priest was going down in that way… ἰδὼν, means to see, perceive, attend to, αὐτὸν, him "derived from the particle αὖ …it applied to what has either been previously mentioned." Bailey argues that the priests were considered among the upper class and most certainly the priest was riding by, when he *comes* to the place, he *saw* the wounded man from a distance. ἀντιπαρῆλθεν, *passes on* the opposite side of the road. Came to him, saw, do nothing, and go.

Verse 32: ὁμοίως, in like manner, similarly, in the same way, equally. It means coincidentally καὶ, and, even, also, namely. Λευίτης, a Levite, a man of the tribe of Levi. Levites are priests' assistants. They were responsible for the liturgy in the temple. Marshall observes that the Levites were considered inferior to the priests but were

---

[92] Bailey, *Through Peasant Eyes*, 42.
[94] Scott, *Hear Then the Parable*, 194.

nevertheless a privileged group in first-century Jewish society.[101] The Levite's response is described in the same manner as the priest's. He *came* to the place and *saw* the wounded man and ἀντιπαρῆλθεν *passed by* on the opposite side. The Levite came, saw, went without action. The same motives are assumed on the part of the Levite to choose not to help the wounded man, although a Levite might be "less bound by ritual requirements than the priest."[103] They—the priest and Levite—both contribute to the wounded man's suffering by their neglect.[104]

The parable makes it clear that the Priest and the Levite were on the road by coincidence. The priest was going κατέβαινεν, down on the road, the same direction, supposedly from Jerusalem to Jericho. Both of them come to the place, do nothing, and go to the other side of the road. But it does not say why they choose to go to the other side of the road when they approach the anonymous half-dead man. "No reason is given, but in the end no reason justifies [their] neglect of the man in need."[105] John Nolland observes that the story's focus is on the priest's failure to help rather than on the reason that he failed to help.[106] Scholars have speculated about the priest's motivations and how a first-century audience would respond to the story. Scott suggests the fear of robbers who may have still been hiding and ready to attack once more.[107] Or perhaps the body on the roadside could have been a plant by robbers to trap a traveler, as Global Bible Commentary suggests.[108] And certainly, the concern of contracting a corpse impurity would be present in the mind of the audience.[109]

Leviticus 21:1-3 spelled out in detail the regulations of the relative corpses that a priest may touch and be considered ceremonially

---

[101] Marshall, *The Gospel of Luke*, 448.
[103] Ibid.
[104] Bailey, *Through Peasant Eyes*, 46.
[105] Leander E. Keck, et. al., eds. *The New Interpreter's Bible: Complete Twelve Volume Commentary, Luke - John* vol. ix (Nashville, TN: Abingdon Press, 1995), 227.
[106] John Nolland, *Luke 9: 21-18: 34, World Biblical Commentary, V35B*, David Hubbard and Glenn W. Barker ed. (Dallas, TX: Word Books Publishers, 1993), 593.
[107] Scott, *Hear Then the Parable*, 195.
[108] Patte, ed., *Global Bible Commentary*, 151.
[109] Scott, *Hear Then the Parable*, 195.

clean. Lev 21: 11 it takes it further, saying that the high priest should not approach any dead person, or defile himself even for his father or his mother. However, despite these strict prohibitions, the Mishnah and Talmud expound some other cases where a high priest and Nazarite may contact a corpse other than their own without the threat of uncleanness, namely a neglected corps (*meth mitzwah*).[110] The Mishnah comments:

> A high priest or a Nazarite may not contract uncleanness because of their [dead] kindred, but they may contract uncleanness because of a neglected corpse. If they were on a journey and found a neglected corpse, Rabbi Eliezer says: The High Priest may contact uncleanness but the Nazarite may not contact uncleanness.[111]

Bauckham expounds the debatable halakhic of the situation a first-century Jewish priest may have found himself in when he encountered a dead or dying man. The situation is one in which two commandments might seem to apply:

> To precisely what circumstances does the commandment to love one's neighbor apply? In what circumstances should I identify someone as the neighbor whom the commandment requires me to love? In response the parable sets up a test-case situation: a priest traveling down the road from Jerusalem to Jericho comes across a man lying half-dead. Should the priest in these circumstances obey the commandment? In these circumstances are the priest and the wounded man defined by the commandment as neighbors, so that the priest should act as a neighbor to the man? Or in these circumstances does the commandment to love one's neighbor not apply, because the priest's obligation to

---

[110] *Meth Mitzwah*, literally meaning, 'a corpse of religious duty,' which means if a corpse was found lying neglected with none to bury it, not among its people Lev. 21, even a high priest must contract uncleanness in order to bury it. Herbert Danby (translator), *The Mishnah: Translated from the Hebrew with Introduction and Brief Explanatory Notes*, (Peabody, MA: Hendrickson Publishers, 2012), 288.

[111] Danby (translator), *The Mishnah*, 289.

another commandment of Torah should take precedence.[112]
Bauckham argues that two commandments are at work in the case of a first-century Jewish priest encountering a man lying half-dead on the road: one which "forbids the priest to contract impurity by contact with a dead body, while the other requires the priest to show neighborly love to the wounded man." Bauckham argues that which of the two obligations would take precedence and override the other, would have depended on the priest's perception of the wounded man's condition. A first-century Jew audience, aware of debatable halakhic, would be profoundly understanding of the priest's personal struggle in trying to be a good man. The struggle is to avoid the sin of defiling himself and attaining sanctity.[115]

On one hand, Bauckham argues that, in any case, the Mishna obliges the priest to help the wounded man whether he dead or alive:

> By the time of the Mishna it as evidently well established in rabbinic *halakhah* that the obligation to bury a *meth mitzwah* takes precedence over the law that priests should not contract corpse-impurity. On this view nothing would impede the priest in the parable from helping the man. If he turned out to be dead, the priest is in any case obliged to defile himself in order to bury him.[116]

On the other, the Samaritan was not obliged to avoid corpse impurity simply because he is not a priest.[117]

Verse 33: The word Σαμαρίτης, means a Samaritan, is an inhabitant either of the city or of the province of Samaria. The Samaritans' sect is a mixed race of the intermarriage between the remnant of the northern ten tribes of Israel and other peoples settled by Shalmaneser, King of Assyria. They accepted belief in God but kept

---

[112] Bauckham, "Scrupulous Priest and the Good Samaritan," 476.
[115] Bailey, *Through Peasant Eyes*, 4.
[116] Bauckham, "Scrupulous Priest and the Good Samaritan," 482.
[117] Ibid.

their idols."[119] (2 Kgs 17) Τις, a certain one, someone, anyone. The wounded man had enjoined two passers-by, the priest and the Levite. The audience is now prepared to expect the third character to be a Jewish layman, which would fit the sequence. This would be someone who is less than a priest and a Levite, not associated with the temple, someone who gives an anti-clerical vantage point to the story, as Marshall observes.[121] Δέ, but a certain Samaritan, for the shock and amazement of the audience, the third one along the road is one who of hated by Jews. He ἦλθεν, comes to, goes to him, and ἰδὼν, sees, perceives, attends to him does something. The most important he felt ἐσπλαγχνίσθη, moved in the inward parts, i.e. to feel compassion.

Verse 34 describes the Samaritan's expression of compassion to the half-dead man. προσελθὼν, to approach, to draw near, he went to him Κατέδησεν, to bind up, τραύματ, wounds by ἐπιχέω, pouring on ἔλαιον, oil and wine. Scott observes that the use of oil and wine as first aid for medical purposes is well attested.[122] Marshall maintains that this part of the story shows certain parallels with the Old Testament story in 2 Chronicles 28: 15.[123] Crossan observes that "Jesus may even have had this case in mind when constructing his own parable."[124] It shows the kindness the people of Samaria showed to their Judean captives. They set them free, "…took the captives, and they clothed all their naked ones from the spoil; and they gave them clothes and sandals, fed them and gave them drink, anointed them with oil, led all their feeble ones on donkeys, and brought them to Jericho, the city of palm trees, to their brothers; then they returned to Samaria." (2 Chronicles 28: 15) The Samaritan ἤγαγεν, brings or carries him, to πανδοχεῖον, an inn and, ἐπεμελήθη took care of him.[126]

---

[119] Zeev Ben-Hayyim, "The Samaritan Pentateuch and the Origin of the Samaritan Sect," *Biblica* 52, no. 2 (1971): 253-255.
[121] Marshall, *The Gospel of Luke*, 449.
[122] Scott, *Hear Then the Parable*, 199.
[123] Marshall, *The Gospel of Luke*, 449.
[124] Crossan, *In Parables*, 65.
[126] All Greek words cited from Strong's Concordance and Greek lexicon.

Bailey observes that the oil and wine were not only standard first-aid remedies, but were also used as sacrificial elements in temple worship.[127] The Samaritan was not obliged to avoid corpse-impurity. However, in contrast to the priest who opts to obey the purity law rather than helping a desperate man in need, the Samaritan gives precedence to the commandment of love over the law of purity.[129] He chooses to move beyond the ritual purity to "steadfast love and not sacrifice." (Hosea 6:6).

Verse 35: The Samaritan took further steps to provide ministration to the wounded man. Taking him to an inn and staying with him through the night, the Samaritan risked his life by allowing himself to be identified to the grieving family of the wounded man. Bailey expounds on the cultural mindset of the Middle Eastern peasant society, that is, "the stranger who involves himself in an accident is often considered partially, if not totally responsible for the accident." Having survived the robbers' attack who may still have been in the area, Bailey suggests that caution should lead him to leave the unconscious wounded man at the door of the inn so he could remain anonymous even to the wounded man.[132]

Verse 36: The word τίς, means who, which of these three do you δοκεῖ, think, to appear, seem γεγονέναι, come into being, to be πλησίον, nearby, a friend, a neighbor to the man who fell into the robbers' hands? (NASB) Again, the lawyer has to answer his question by choosing the one who *acted* neighborly. Jesus thus avoided the theological argument. Crossan argues that this question would serve as an excellent conclusion for the original parable.[134]

Verse 37: The word ἔλεος means the lawyer answers the question, the one who had ποιήσας, shown ἔλεος, mercy, pity, compassion on him. His answer shows his reluctance to name the Samaritan. The answer should simply be, the Samaritan. Instead, he

---

[127] Bailey, *In the Eyes of Peasants*, 50.
[129] Bauckham, "Scrupulous Priest and the Good Samaritan," 479.
[132] Bailey, *In the Eyes of Peasants*, 52.
[134] Crossan, *In Parables*, 61.

avoids naming the despised Samaritan. Marshall observes that, "by his answer he shows that being neighborly means showing mercy."[136] Again, Crossan argues that the answer does not change the content of the parable. He maintains that the lawyer's answer would make no difference to the parable's interpretation, even if it were original.[137]

Jesus said to him go and Ποίει, DO, ACT, cause ὁμοίως, in like manner. Bailey argues that instead of telling the lawyer who is and who is not his neighbor, he reshapes the lawyer's question to: "To whom must you become a neighbor?" Bailey notes Jesus' last statement "is not a general admonition to good works but rather an answer to the lawyer's question about self-justification." He maintains "the first round of question and answers ended with a command to DO something. This round ends in the same manner."[139]

Overcoming Cultural and Religious Prejudice

The question is, how does Jesus parable sound to a first-century Middle-Eastern audience? How does it sound to Luke's readers who inferred the man was non-Jewish? What kind of hero does the audience expect in the parable of the Good Samaritan? Who, in the end, proved to be the neighbor to the man who fell into the robbers' hands? Richard Bauckham argues that the question, "who is my neighbor?" was a typical question of the *halakhic* discussions among first-century Judaism. It is a question about the correct interpretations of the commandment. He suggests that the parable is Jesus' distinctive interpretation of the Law of Moses.[141] Jesus narrates the parable as an answer to the question: who is the neighbor I should love?, which commandment should I follow—the impurity contract or the love commandment?.

Why did Luke think that the lawyer wanted to justify himself by asking for a definition? Was the lawyer convinced that, whatever

---

[136] Marshall, *The Gospel of Luke*, 450.
[137] Crossan, *In Parables*, 61.
[139] Bailey, *In the Eyes of Peasants*.
[141] Bauckham, "Scrupulous Priest and the Good Samaritan," 447.

Jesus response, no way would he have it all? How would the lawyer react if Jesus reversed his point with a Jew finding an injured Samaritan? In a devout society such as the Middle-Eastern context, where the cloak of religion is draped over all actions and thoughts in everyday live, how can we apply the concept of the Good Samaritan today? Needless to say that the issue is not the sacred texts themselves, it is our interpretation, understanding, and application. Bauckham concludes his article, "Jesus' Interpretation of the Law of Moses," by arguing that Jesus does not use the parable to satirize the Jewish religious establishment of the priesthood. He maintains that Jesus' parable's "issue is how the law should be interpreted and therefore obeyed."[142]

Jesus responded to the Pharisees' criticism of not observing the law and tradition by saying "…go and learn what this means: 'I desire compassion, and not sacrifice." (Matthew 9:13) The Samaritan extended his sympathy to someone he does not know—a certain man who was desperate for help. By extending a helping hand to a wounded man by the side of the road, he made the non-neighbor a real neighbor. He took the initiative by risking his life to approach him, and through this compassionate action he became neighbor. If that same person had been encountered alive and well, instead of stripped, beaten, and half-dead, he would have shown the Samaritan rejection, indignation, and contempt, rather than kindness and respect.[144] To such an enemy, the Samaritan felt compassion. Donahue notes that, "in the parable, the Samaritan is not converted and thus remains an 'enemy,' so that gone is the apocalyptic vision of ultimate triumph over one's enemy. The world with its sure arrangement of insiders and outsiders is no longer an adequate model for predicting the kingdom."[145]

---

[142] Bauckham, "Scrupulous Priest and the Good Samaritan," 488.
[144] Tokunboh Adeyemo, ed. *Africa Bible Commentary,* 1st edition (Grand Rapids, MI: World Alive Publishers, Zondervan, 2006), 1225.
[145] Donahue, "Who Is My Enemy?" 144.

On the other hand, the priest and Levite behaved unneighborly. They did nothing to help their fellow Israelite, to whom, in a daily life situation, they would have behaved neighborly. Robert A. J. Gagnon observes that the parable enables the hearer to perceive the enemy as a potential neighbor in one's moment of distress and so make it easier to love such a one.[146] By narrating the Good Samaritan parable, "Jesus challenges both the historical reality of viewing the Samaritan as enemy and the deeper religious attitude that divides the world into outsiders and insiders."[147]

Can We Come Together to Learn about The Other?

The initial admonition of "the Common Word Letter" is to set an interfaith dialogue among Muslim, Christian, and all people of goodwill on the academic and religious level. George Malek discusses the characteristics of how the sort of Christian-Muslim interreligious dialogue in the Middle East should be. He argues that kind of dialogue should "not [be] in terms of scholarly pursuits nor academic understanding but terms of sincere, practical exchanges of religious attitudes." He set two principles. The first is of a Christian nature, namely, Christ's commandment to "Love your neighbor as yourself." The second is of an Islamic nature, whereby Allah commands Muslims to "come to common terms as between You [the people of the book] and Us [Muslims]: that we worship none but Allah (Al-I-Imran; 3:64)..."[149]

This dialogue should not just be in the religious and academic levels. It should be in everyday life situations where we can break down the walls of mistrust, disrespect, and dislike of each other. We have to stop dehumanizing, demonizing, despising, and attacking each other.

---

[146] Robert A J. Gagnon, "A Second Look at Two Lukan Parables: Reflections on the Unjust Steward and the Good Samaritan," in *Horizons in Biblical Theology* 20, No. 1 (June, 1998), 1-11.

[147] Donahue, "Who Is My Enemy?" 144.

[149] George N. Malek, "Christian-Muslim dialogue," *Missiology* 16, no. 3 (July, 1988), 279.

We must break the fear, insecurity, prejudices, bigotry, and the wall of rejection that separates, and build instead bridges of trust, respect, and understanding, where people can comfortably and respectfully converse about spiritual matters with those of other faiths.[150]

The Parable as Missio-Logos Inter-Religious Dialogue [151]

In his article "Missio-logoi, Interreligious Dialogue, and the Parable of the Good Samaritan," Terry Muck argues that, although the parable of the Good Samaritan has the elements characteristic of an interreligious exchange, that is, interaction among Jews and Samaritans, he observes that commentators never picked up on the meaning of the parable from that point of view—the interreligious dialogue.[152] Muck looks at three readings of the parable. He argues that traditionally the parable of the Good Samaritan "has been interpreted using either an exegetical method focusing on allegory or a method focusing on the ethical content of the text." He maintains that "the earliest interpretations were heavily weighted toward the allegorical and later interpretations were weighted toward the ethical."[154]

Muck argues that there are three readings[155] emerge from the commentarial literature that is the ethical identity reading, soteriological reading, and the ecclesiological reading. The three readings differ according to three questions the reader tends to focus on: What must I do to be saved?; Who is my neighbor?; or Which of these do you think is a neighbor to the man robbed and beaten?[157] Muck maintains, "by focusing on one or the other of these three

---

[150] Barry E. Hughes, "Love Your Neighbor? Christian/Muslim Relations as A Way of Fulfilling the Great Commandment," (DMin dissertation, United Theological Seminary, 2005), 5.

[151] *Missio-logos*, as Muck defines it, is a language used to describe the mission implications of a text.

[152] Terry C. Muck, "Missio-logoi, interreligious dialogue, and the parable of the Good Samaritan," *Missiology* 44, No. 1 (January, 2016), 5-19, 8.

[154] Muck, "Missio-logoi.," 9.

[155] The reading is that all are ways of approaching the text: such as exegesis, interpretation, and criticism.

[157] Muck, "Missio-logoi," 10.

questions, different sets of words, images, and metaphors emerge, that is, different *missio-logoi*. Consider each in turn." The first reading is soteriological, focusing on the question, "What must I do to be saved?" Muck argues that the reader uses the *missio-logos* to the parable as a clear answer, "Go and do as the Samaritan did in the story," to the lawyer's question, "What must I do to be saved?"[159]

The second, the ethical reading, focuses on the parable as Jesus' answer to the lawyer's question, "Who is my neighbor?" Muck argues that throughout the parable, Jesus is "advocating universal reconciliation. Everyone is my neighbor, even people of different ethnic backgrounds, even people belonging to different religious traditions. All can/must love God and neighbor as self."[160]

The third is the ecclesiological reading, focusing on the question, "Which of these do you think is a neighbor to the man robbed and beaten?" According to Muck, "God's kingdom is not made up of the strong and self-sufficient, but of the weak and needy who have come to see their neediness and all ready to be helped—even by Samaritans."[161] Muck maintains, "we all lay in our own ditches and need God and one another." He argues that this reading is a modern modification to the traditional interpretation that changes the identity of the characters of the parable the same way that Augustine allegorizes them.[163] Muck observes that Jesus' lesson to the inquisitive lawyer and the Jewish listeners is, "if a member of a hated religious group, the Samaritans, can behave like this to members of the other religious groups, so should we, no matter what our respective religions."[164]

Muck concludes his article by providing an answer to the question, "What kind of reading of the parable of the Good Samaritan

---

[159] Ibid.
[160] Ibid.
[161] Ibid, 11.
[163] Ibid.
[164] Ibid.

do we get when we use the *missio-logos* of interreligious dialogue?" He responds by raising three sub-questions.

First he asks, "when we use the *missio-logos* of the interreligious dialogue to read the parable, do we get an accurate, faithful reading?" His answer is yes. Muck maintains that the Good Samaritan parable contains two essential characteristics of the interreligious texts that is the first characteristic that is there is two different religions are involved in the parable; the Jewish religion and the other is different what it calls the Samaritan religion. The second characteristic is the interaction among the two religions involved whether is positive or negative.[166]

Second, in his responding to the question: Is the reading useful within the Christian community? Muck argues that such reading seems to inflame the existing interreligious and intrareligious tensions; interreligious, it seems exacerbate the tension between Christians and Jews as it displays "the Jews in the story did not rise to the occasion of being 'good Samaritans.'" Also it seems exacerbate the intrareligious tension within the Christian mission community itself. The tension that has arisen regarding the mode of the interaction with the non-Christian whether it should be evangelization or dialogue. The division comes from considering which is proper and which is not, "the primacy of either proclamation of the gospel versus social action, that is, care for the poor, sick, and dying." However, ultimately, Muck believes that an interreligious reading, among others, would be acceptable to the Christian mission community. It "could contribute to reconciliation, especially regarding mission goals within the Christian mission community."[167]

Third, in addressing the question: "Is the interreligious reading useful as a tool in the work of doing mission?" Muck argues that the interreligious dialogical reading of the parable would be useful, especially in cultures that confront classical Christianity. Muck provides

---

[166] Ibid, 14.
[167] Ibid,15.

practical, missiological, theological, and commonsensical reasons for an interreligious dialogical reading, such as that this type of reading is useful in Islamic countries where mission takes the form of social concern in the name of Christ. The missiological reason is that the "care of the sick and injured is an essential part of doing Christian mission."[169] The theological reason is that the parable demonstrates the biblical way to relate to people of other religions.[170] The parable demonstrates what it means to be Christians in a religiously plural society, and demonstrates the need in this context of a loving God, loving neighbors, even loving enemies. The commonsensical reason is our common humanity and our need for loving care that trumps religious differences.[171]

Conclusion

In this chapter, we looked at the first-century bigotry and prejudice relationship between the Jews and the Samaritans while the enmity was at its highest point after the Samaritans desecrated the temple with human bones. We looked at the debatable halakhic of the situation a first-century Jewish priest may have found himself in when he encountered a dead or dying man. In this historical context, by giving the parable of the Good Samaritan Jesus offered a new understanding of the commandment to love the neighbor. Jesus wanted to help the lawyer instead of asking who is or he is not neighbor; he reshapes the lawyer's question to: To whom he must become a neighbor?

The search looked at the different readings of the parable. One of these reading is the interreligious reading. Terry Muck sheds light on the use of the interreligious reading of the parable as a tool in the work of doing the mission especially in cultures that confront classical Christianity. One of the uses of this type of reading is useful in Islamic countries where the mission takes the form of social concern in the

---

[169] Ibid.
[170] Ibid, 16.
[171] Ibid,16.

name of Christ "care of the sick and injured is an essential part of doing Christian mission." The parable also demonstrates what it means to be Christians in a religiously plural society, and demonstrates the need in this context of a loving God, loving neighbors, even loving enemies.

For centuries, Arab Christians embrace righteous indignation on one hand, and, on the other, the Islamic culture has instilled fear and ill-will on them. As a result, Middle-Eastern Christians tend to allow fear to prevent them from loving their Muslim neighbors. Being socially and politically marginalized, Middle Eastern Christians developed psychological ghettos for themselves as a harbor of fear. The Samaritan in Jesus' parable is a good example of risking life and sacrificing time, effort, and resources as well as renouncing the enmity and go beyond his righteous indignation to help someone who supposed to be his enemy.

In his article "Applied Spirituality in Ministry Among Muslims," Phil Parshall comments on a painting of a ship that waits in the harbor to be released. He notes the inscription on the pictures states: "A ship in a harbor is safe, but that is not what ships are built for."[173] "The spiritual Christian does not ghettoize his faith in a harbor of like-minded believers where all is safe and calm—but rather, courageously puts forth his ship into the sea of life where danger, difficulty, and distress abound. This is what "spiritual ships" are built for."[174]

The example of the Good Samaritan must be consciously in the mind of the Christian at all times, as Francis Schaeffer suggests. He wrote, "Christians are not to love their believing brothers to the exclusion of their non-believing fellowmen."[175] As followers of Jesus, Christians have to overcome all the barriers of intolerance, prejudice, racism, and contempt to reach out to their neighbors. Christian faith is

---

[173] Phil Parshall, "Applied Spirituality in Ministry among Muslims," *Missiology* 11, no. 4 (October 1983): 435-447.

[174] Parshall, "Applied Spirituality."

[175] Francis Schaeffer, *The Mark of the Christian*, Abridged Edition.

like a ship built to endure the strongest impact from the stormy seas. It is built to harbor in the rough and stormy seas of life. This is what Christians are called for.

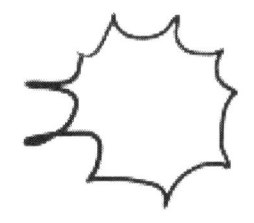

Chapter Three

Muslims and Christians Interaction: A Historical Model

Introduction

The historical literature coming from the past, especially in the field of inter-religious dialogue in the Middle Eastern context, can give us insight into our present situation, and possibly even make a positive contribution to our human future. This literature reminds us that the peaceful co-existence between Islam, Christianity, and Judaism are possible. Love for our neighbor today, in a fraught atmosphere, one filled with a long history of divisiveness and hostility, requires a study of the history. In his book, *Doing Church History: A User-friendly Introduction to Researching the History of Christianity,* Gordon L. Heath quotes George Marsden (a historian whose work focuses on the interplay between Christianity and American culture, particularly as it pertains to higher education and evangelicalism) about why Christians should teach and learn history:

> The basic reason why we who are Christians should teach and learn history is so that we may better

understand ourselves and our fellow men in relation to our culture and to the world. Since the Christian's task is to live in this world and to witness to the love of God as manifested in Christ, it is essential for us to understand ourselves and the world as best we can. Love is the Christian's central obligation, and understanding is an essential ingredient in love. If we are going to love others. it seems evident that we should try our best to understand them.[1]

Heath continues his study about why doing church history matters, saying:

A study of church's history also frees it to try new things in new ways. Why? A study of the past shows that there has been numerous ways in which things have been done, and there have been countless innovative methods of reaching cultures for Christ.[2]

Heath lists the history of apologetics as one reason we should commit ourselves to learning as much as possible about the church's history. Heath writes:

How does one begin to address hostile claims about the church past when one does not even know the past? To be ignorant of the church's history is to place yourself in the unenviable position of having to defend or explain the past without even knowing much or anything about it.[3]

In *The Legacy of Arab-Islam in Africa: A Quest for Inter-Religious Dialogue,* John Alembillah Azumah argues that documenting and interpreting the history of the inter-religious dialogue between people of different religious traditions, and between Christian and Muslims, in

---

[1] George M. Marsden, "A Christian Perspective for the Teaching of History," *A Christian View of History?* George Marsden and Frank Roberts, ed. (Grand Rapids, MI: William B. Eerdmans Publishing Company, 1975), 31, 32.

[2] Gordon L. Heath, *Doing Church History: A User-friendly Introduction to Researching the History of Christianity* (Ontario, Canada: Clements Publishing, 2008), 28.

[3] Heath, *Doing Church History*, 28.

particular, became more than an academic duty; it is a sacred one. Azumah writes:

> The call to take history seriously is therefore crucial if we are to understand appreciate and better deal with contemporary inter-religious difficulties, tension and conflicts. Taking history seriously will also help us learn the necessary lessons from the historical encounters and charting a path for better relations in the future. This means that the documentation and interpretation of what actually happened in the past is more than just an academic exercise. In a sense, it is a sacred duty.[4]

Studying the history of the inter-religious dialogue between Christian and Muslims helps us adequately understand Muslim beliefs and their interactions with Christians.

Additionally, studying biographies of Christian leaders can teach us lessons about how they thrived under the pressure of Islam. *Mans u r ibn Sarju n*, grandfather of John of Damascus[5], participated in the negotiations for the capitulation of Damascus and then became head of *Mu'a wiya's* tax administration. *Sarju n's* grandson, *Mans u r*, was born and grew up as a Christian under Islamic rule. He lived in Islamic culture and served on the court of the Islamic Umayyad court until he joined the ranks of the church and took the name John of Damascus after the death of *'Abd al-Malik*.[6] Timothy, the Patriarch of Baghdad, led the East church to thrive under the rule of the Abbasid Caliphs in the late eighth and early ninth centuries. Timothy risked his life and a hanging death, relinquishing fear while facing difficult faith questions. These are just two of many examples of Christian leaders

---

[4] John Alembillah Azumah, *The Legacy of Arab-Islam in Africa: A Quest for Inter-Religious Dialogue* (London, UK: Oneworld Publications, 2014), preface.

[5] John of Damascus, (born c. 675, Damascus—died Dec. 4, 749, near Jerusalem) eastern monk and theological doctor of the Greek and Latin churches whose treatises on the veneration of sacred images placed him in the forefront of the 8th-century Iconoclastic Controversy, and whose theological synthesis made him a preeminent intermediary between Greek and medieval Latin culture."

[6] Arietta Papaconstantinou, "Between *umma* and *dhimma*: The Christians of the Middle East under the *Umayyads*," *Annales islamologiques* (42) 2008, 136.

who could teach and inspire us in the twenty-first century.

Such historical studies are essential for helping the church understand itself and its relationship to the world. They instruct Christians on their responsibility towards their non-Christian relatives, friends, neighbors, and toward the whole non-Christian community.[7] It is essential to address these questions to impact the church in the twenty-first century, and in the Arabic Christian context in particular. Christians must work to shed the heavy cultural baggage of fear and intimidation, and follow their great predecessors in loving their neighbors.

The research in this first section will consider the legacy of Patriarch Timothy I as a model of the dialogical approach of Medieval Middle Eastern Christianity, known for its defense of the Christian faith. Then, the apology of Patriarch Timothy I of Baghdad before Caliph Mahdi will be examined in depth as a historical foundation for this project. The apology considers one of the oldest inter-religious Arabic apologies for Christianity. According to Samir K. Samir, "the apology took place in 781 EC. But the *aide mémoire* of the debate, written by Timothy himself in a letter to the monk Sergios and published by Dr. Alphonse Mingana in Syriac."[8] This project employs the English translation, *The Apology of Timothy the Patriarch before the Caliph Mahdi,* in "Woodbrooke Studies; Christian documents in Syriac, Arabic, and Garshuni." Also consulted is the debate in Samir K. Samir's critical edition of the Arabic.[9]

---

[7] John R. W. Stott, *Christian Mission in the Modern World: What the Church Should Be Doing Now,* (Downers Grove, Ill: Intervarsity Press, 1975), 11.

[8] Samir Khalil Samir, S.J., "The Earliest Arab Apology for Christianity (C. 750)," in *Christian Arabic Apologetics during the Abbasid Period (750-1258),* edited by Samir Khalil Samir, and Jorgen S. Nelsen. LXIII, 57–114 (Leiden, Netherlands: E. J. Brill, 1994), 63.

[9] Clint Hackenburg, "An Arabic-to-English Translation of the Religious Debate between the Nestorian Patriarch Timothy I and the 'Abbāsid Caliph al-Mahdī," (master's thesis, The Ohio State University, 2009).

Patriarch Timothy I of Baghdad (780-823)

Timothy was born in 727 in the village of H azza near Adiabene. He attended the monastic school in Bas ōš, a small village in northern Mesopotamia. There he studied Greek and Arabic.[10] Frederick W. Norris argues that Timothy was born and raised in a wealthy Christian family and was well-educated both in theology and Greek philosophy. This made him a good fit for Baghdad, a cosmopolitan city:

> Born into a wealthy family, he was sent by his uncle George, a bishop, for initial schooling in the Bible to the revered Rabban Mar Abraham the Expositor. Under him he learned the interpretive skills ... Later Timothy was introduced to Greek philosophy, more hermeneutics as well as theology, and probably medicine at the 'mother of patriarchs and bishops,' the famous Adiabene monastery Bet Abe (south of Mosul, Iraq.)[11]

In the *Book of the Governors* by Thomas Bishop of Marga, there is a prophecy made by an old monk who lived in Beth Beghash Monastery concerning the young man, Timothy. According to Thomas, the boy's uncle, who was the Bishop of *Bet Baghash*, sent Timothy to *Rabban Mar Abraham* when he was in a monastery in *Bashosh*. An old man came to this community and saw the young man. He took Timothy to his cell, asked him to sit down, and eventually admonished him saying:

> Go now and buy wheat, and eat, and work fully in the study of the scriptures, and guard yourself from all ignoble things, for thou shalt become Patriarch of all the country of the East. And behold, our Lord will make thee triumphant so that like unto thee no one hath ever been, and before and after thee no one shall

---

[10] Hackenburg, "An Arabic-to-English Translation," 4.
[11] Frederick W. Norris, "Timothy I of Baghdad, Catholicos of the East Syrian Church, 780-823: Still a Valuable Model," *International Bulletin of Missionary Research* 30, no. 3 (July 1, 2006), 133-136.

> ever be. Forty [p. 196] and two years shalt thou stand at the head of all the pastures of Christ, and when by the hand of God thou hast been exalted to these things, let thy heart be disposed to honor this holy house, in which it was [made] known to thee that thou wert neither of no account nor despised before Go; go now in peace and keep those things which I have commanded thee. [12]

Timothy was considered to be one of the most prominent patriarchs in the history of the Church of the East.[13] In his book, *the Church of the East: A Concise History*, Wilhelm Baum states:

> Timothy I (780-823) came to office through simony but developed into one of the most important ecclesiastical writers and most capable organizers of the Apostolic Church of the East, which by then extended into India and China. [Timothy] was elected after an eight-month vacancy of the patriarchal seat; his ordination in May 780.[14]

At the time, the patriarch was elected by the bishops then ratified by the caliph. In 762, Timothy transferred the residence of the Catholicos from *Ctesiphon*, the capital of the Sasanian Empire, to the newly founded city of Baghdad, and he settled in a monastery of the Catholicos called, in Arabic, *Deir al-Jathaliq*.[15]

Although the Pact of Umar prohibited Christians from erecting new churches or monasteries, "Timothy was able to persuade the Caliph to allow him to repair churches and to send church planters to former 'Christian' lands then under Muslim rule."[16] Norris observes that by the late of eighth century, Timothy was able to plant congregations in Syria, Palestine, Asia Minor, Cyprus, and Egypt.

---

[12] Thomas Bishop of Marga, *The Book of Governors*, edited by Ernest Alfred Wallis Budge, *Google EBooks*, Vol. 2. (London, UK: K. Paul, Trench, Trübner & Company, Ltd., 1893), Book 4, 381, digitized by *the University of Michigan*, April 13, 2006.

[13] Budge, ed., *The Book of Governors*, 381.

[14] Ibid, 60.

[15] Dale T. Irvin, and Scott W. Sunquist. *History of the World Christian Movement* (New York, NY: Orbis Books, 2001), 284.

[16] Norris, "Timothy I of Baghdad," 133.

Norris argues that the East Syrian experience in the eighth century spread from Cypress to China because the East Syrian church in Persia had neither been a constant irritant to Muslims nor been a part of the Christian religion under the Byzantines. However, throughout the article, Norris argues that neither Timothy nor the story of his church did take the intention it should be as a standard model to be taught in church history classes.[17]

The Abbasids

The Abbasid Dynasty, the decent of Abbas, they claimed descent from Muhammad through Muhammad's uncle, Abbas.[18] The Abbasid Dynasty came to power as a result of a civil war between the rival faction of the house of the Prophet Muhammad; this has customarily been referred to as the Abbasid revolution.[19] The Abbasid became the third Muslim Caliphate after Muhammad . After consolidating their rule with Baghdad as the new capital of the Caliphate, the Abbasids continued to grant a privileged position to the Nestorian as the preferred Christians. The role that has been assumed by the Sasanians for many years.[20] Unlike the Umayyads, the Abbasids revived the Persian culture; arts, poetry, and science flourished in Baghdad. The Abbasids also learned from the Chinese soldiers captured in battle the art of making paper, which became an important material for spreading literature and knowledge.[21]

The Abbasids sponsored the translation movement initiated by Al Mansur, the first Caliph (754 – 775 AD), and it lasted two centuries. This contributed to the translation of ancient Greek scientific and cultural books into Arabic. The Syriac-speaking Christians, with the

---

[17] Ibid..
[18] "History of Ancient Civilization, The Abbasid Dynasty: The Golden Age of Islamic Civilization," online courses by the Saylor Foundation.
[19] Dimitri Gutas, *Greek Thought, Arabic Culture: The Graeco-Arabic Translation Movement in Baghdad and Early 'Abbasaid Society (2nd-4th/ 5th-10th C.*, (London, UK and New York, NY: Routledge, 2012), 28.
[20] Hackenburg, "An Arabic-to-English Translation," 2.
[21] "History of Ancient Civil

patronage of the caliphs, played a fundamental role in the transmission of Greek science to Muslim scholarship.[22] There were famous Christians scholars such as *Hunayn ib´n Ishaq* (809-873).[23]

Abu Abdullah Muhammad ibn Abdullah al-Mansur, known by his regnal name al-Mahdi. Al-Mahdi was the third caliph of the Abbasid monarchies. The apology of Timothy before Mahdi was one of the Christians and the emerging Islamic Anti-Trinitarian polemics took place 781, nearly a century and a half after the Islamic invasion of Iraq. The Arab attack to the east part of the Arabia started by Muhammad's successor, Abu Bakr within a decade of Muhammad's death in 632. Then Umar ibn al-Khattab, Abu-Bakr's successor extended Muslim power throughout Arabia Peninsula. The same happened in the western regions of the Persian Empire, in major cities in the Byzantine, such as Damascus and Jerusalem. This brought the Sassanian Dynasty to an end and the second Muslim's caliphate, the Umayyad. Then, emerged the Abbasids overthrew the second caliphate and moved their capital city of the Islamic empire from Damascus to Baghdad. Baghdad was founded in 762 by al-Mansur.[24] Soon Baghdad became the largest city in the world under the rule of the Abbasid Dynasty.

The Text in its Context

Christian apologetic literature emerged out of necessity because Arab Christians found themselves in an Islamic culture, facing anti-Christian polemic, with theological accusations that Christians were polytheists. Christian apologetics was a popular literary genre in the Abbasside period. The Christian *Mutakallim,*[25] oral response (Lit. utterer), appears at the caliph's court, defending the Christian faith in

---

[22] Gutas, *Greek Thought, Arabic Culture*, 3.
[23] John F. Healey, "The Syriac-Speaking Christians and the Translation of Greek Science into Arabic," in *Muslim Heritage*.
[24] "History of Ancient Civilization," 2.
[25] 'Ilm al-Kalām, (Lit. Since of speech or utterance) is one of the "religious sciences" of Islam. Gardet, L., "'Ilm al-Kalām", in *Encyclopedia of Islam*, 2nd Ed., Edited by P. Bearman, Th. Bianquis, C.E. Bosworth, E. van Donzel, W.P. Heinrichs.

response to the questions posed by the caliph himself or on his behalf."[26] Later in the in the ninth century (third century of the Islamic calendar)[27] this type of anti-Islamic polemic came to be called Christian *Mujadilun,* disputers. The Mujadilun were philosophical-minded Christians who began to respond in written logical apologies as a direct response to the Islamic disputes.[28] S. Griffith adds another reason for the rise of this kind of literature: as a response to a campaign that began in the Abbasid Empire to convert Christians.[29] On the one hand they had to refute Islamic theological assertions of being polytheists. On the other, they had to validate their Christian faith in a contextual theology.

The debate is one of the early important Islamic-Christian dialogues. It occurred between two prominent leaders: Timothy, the Patriarch of the Eastern Church, and el-Mahdi, the Abbasid caliph. The debate demonstrates Timothy's audacity as a Christian *Mutakallim.* The apology is the output of the second of the two-day interreligious dialogue with the Abbasid caliph.[30] It survived in a Syriac letter, written by Timothy to an anonymous correspondent, widely believed to be Bishop Sergius, in the city of Elam.[31] Besides the apology of Timothy from the eighth century, there are surviving works of a trio famous

---

[26] Sidney H. Griffith, "Faith and Reason in Christian Kalam: *Theodore Abu Qurrah* on Discerning the True Religion," pp 1-43. *Christian Arabic Apologetics During the Abbasid Period (750-1258)* edited by Samir Khalil Samir, and Jorgen S. Nelsen. LXIII. (E. J. Brill: Leiden, Netherland, 1994), 5.

[27] The Islamic Calendar (Hijri), Or Hijri calendar is a lunar calendar consisting of 12 months in a year of 354 or 355 days, reckoned from the year of the Hegira in ad 622, Muhammad's emigration to Madina.

[28] Gabriel Said Reynolds, "A Muslim Theologian in the Sectarian Milieu: 'Abd Al-Jabbār and the Critique of Christian Origins," in *Islamic History and Civilization*, Volume 56. (Leiden, Netherlands: Brill, 2004), 228.

[29] Reynolds, "A Muslim Theologian," 228.

[30] J. Coakley and A. Sterk, ed., "Early Medieval Christianity in Asia. 45. Apology of Patriarch Timothy of Baghdad before the Caliph Mahdi," in *Readings in World Christian History: V1: Earliest Christianity to 1453*, 11th ed. (Maryknoll, NY: Orbis, 2012), 231-242, 231.

[31] Hackenburg, "An Arabic-to-English Translation," 3.

scholars from the ninth century: Abu Qurrah (d. 204/820), Abu Ra'ita (d. early-mid ninth entury), Amar al-Basri (d. 260/874).[32]

The Content

The apology[33] is in a polemical literature format—question and answer. It is Timothy's answers to the questions the caliph has raised. Timothy begins his apology by showing the necessary respect to the caliph. It is evident that the dialogue occurred in a high level of intimacy, friendship, and mutual respect. Timothy addresses the caliph by superlative expression such as "King of Kings" or "our God-loving King" or "his exalted Majesty." The caliph addresses Timothy as the "Catholicos." Norris suggests that Timothy "went under the protection of [al]-majils, a type of decree that encouraged those invited to the caliph palace to talk freely about whatever they knew of their religion and Islam without any threat of death."[34] Timothy shows himself to be a masterful, wise, and bold. He showed sincere respect. He also maintained self-respect, never swerving from his purpose of maintaining what he believes is right. Timothy used philosophical, theological, scriptural, and logical tools, presenting sound arguments to persuade the caliph of the validity of the Christian faith.

The caliph raised the common stereotypes that most Muslims held about the Christian faith at that time. The caliph questioned the source of the Bible and maintained the Muslim allegation that the Bible was distorted by Christians. He also questioned the Christology issues: the deity of Christ and the question of how God had a human son. The caliph questioned how God could be one and three at the same

---

[32] Reynolds, "A Muslim Theologian," 218.

[33] Apology, autobiographical form in which a defense is [a] framework for a discussion by the author of his personal beliefs and viewpoints. An early example dating from the 4th century BC is Plato's Apology, a philosophical dialogue dealing with the trial of Socrates, in which Socrates answers the charges of his accusers by giving a brief history of his life and his moral commitment. Such an apology is usually a self-justification. *Encyclopedia Britannica.*

[34] Norris, "Timothy I of Baghdad," 135.

time. For Muslims, Jesus is a mere human being, a good man, sinless, and a great prophet of God, but with no divine dimensions. Moreover, Muslims do not believe in Jesus' crucifixion. They struggle with why Christians worship the cross. If Jesus is God, why did God suffer? Why would God have allowed his prophet to be crucified?

Another stereotype concerns the source of the Qur'an and Muhammad's prophethood. What do Christians say about the Qur'an? Was it revealed by God? What do Christians say about Muhammad? Was he the seal of prophets? What about Moses' prophecy in Deuteronomy 18:18? The caliph asked, "who is the one who is said to have been seen riding a camel?"[35] He reinterpreted Isaiah's prophecy as a reference to Muhammad. Furthermore, he asked: "Who is then the Paraclete? Is he not Muhammad?"[36] He believed that the Torah, the Prophets, and even Christ testify to Muhammad's prophethood, but that Christians do not accept the testimony of Christ and the Gospel regarding Muhammad. The caliph even desperately asked two times, "have you not received any? Timothy's answer was: "No, I have not received any." This ended by charging Christians of corrupting their own scriptures and suppressing the testimonies of Muhammad, so that there is no proof of Muhammad's prophethood. The caliph states, "There were many testimonies but the Books have been corrupted, and you have removed them."[37]

The Allegations of Torah and the Gospel Corruption

Timothy responded to the caliph's question about the source of the Bible by saying that the Bible and the Torah are the Word of God received by the Prophets and the apostles of Jesus from God, just as Muslims believe that Muhammad received the Qur'an from an angel.

---

[35] Hackenburg, "An Arabic-to-English Translation," 19.
[36] *The Apology of Timothy the Patriarch before the Caliph Mahdi, Wood Brooke Studies, Christians in Syriac, Arabic, and Garshuni* edited and translated with critical apparatus by Alphonse Mingana, V. 2. 26-338, 33.
[37] Mingana, *Apology of Timothy the Patriarch*, 35.

Timothy responded to the allegation that the Books (the Torah and the Gospel) have been corrupted by Christians by counter-questions:

> Where is it known, Oh King, that the books have been corrupted by us, and where that uncorrupted Book from which you have learned that the Books which we use have been corrupted? If there is such a book let it be placed in the middle in order that we may learn from which is the corrupted Gospel and hold to that which is not corrupted. If there is no such a Gospel, how do you know that the Gospel of which we make use is corrupted? What possible gain could we have gathered from corrupting the Gospel? Even if there was mention of Muhammad made in the Gospel, we would not have deleted his name from it; we would simply said that Muhammad has not come yet, and that was not the one whom you follow, and that he was going to come in the future.[38]

The Christology

The initial question posed by the caliph was whether Timothy and the Christians believed that God the Most High took a woman for companionship and begat from her a son. Timothy denies this allegation of the biological connection between God and Jesus via Mary.[39] Mahdi retorted: "Do you not say that Christ is the Son of God?"[40] Timothy makes a distinction between the eternal Sonship of the Word-God who appeared in the flesh and the temporal birth. He states that:

> The very same Christ is the Word born of the Father before the times, as light from the sun and word from the soul; and … he is man. He is born of the Virgin Mary, in time; from the Father, he is therefore, born

---

[38] Hackenburg, "An Arabic-to-English Translation," 86.
[39] I. Mark Beaumont, *Christology in Dialogue with Muslims: A Critical Analysis of Christian Presentations of Christ for Muslims from the Ninth and Twentieth Centuries* (Eugene, OR: Wipf and Stock Publishers, 2011), 23.
[40] Mingana, *Apology of Timothy the Patriarch*, 17.

eternally, and from the mother he is born in time without a father, without any martial contact.[41]

The caliph argues that there are, therefore, two distinct beings, two Christs: one created and fashioned and the other uncreated and unfashioned. Timothy responded the Word-God "is one with his humanity, while preserving the distinction between his invisibility and his visibility, and between his divinity and humanity. Christ is one in his Son-ship, and two in the attributes of his nature. To prove his thesis that Christ has one sonship in two attributes of his nature, Timothy uses the analogy of one tongue with the word and the voice, the one does not expel the two. Another illustration Timothy uses is the king's letter. The letter is comprised of both the written words and the papyrus, however the king is called both the father and the owner of his letter.[42]

Timothy admitted that the eternal birth of the Word-God cannot be comprehended by the mere mind, nor can it be expressed in words. He states "but [Christ's] birth is not like the bodily birth, rather it is a miraculous birth, beyond the comprehension of the mind and description of the tongue as is befitting for the divine birth."[43] However the caliph still had a hard time comprehending the two births. He asked, "How can the spirit who has no genital organs beget?" Timothy's response is, "as [God] created the worlds without instruments of creation, so [the son] was born without the medium of the genital organs." Again Timothy uses the analogy of the sun. It begets the rays of the light without any genital organs; God, therefore, begets the son and makes the spirit proceed from the essence of his person.

The conversation shows two approaches to Christ's two births and two natures— reason and faith. The caliph appeals to logic, reason, and common sense. The caliph questioned Timothy's argumentation that the Eternal One was born in time. He also argued that it is

[41] Ibid.
[42] Ibid, 21.
[43] Hackenburg, "An Arabic-to-English Translation," 43.

logically impossible to integrate two natures in one person and insisted that this would be two beings, two Christs. Conversely, Timothy appealed to the scripture as well as the theological, philosophical concepts, and natural explanations. He argued that Christ is One Person in two *hupostasis* (hypostasis), neither separated nor divided. However, Mahdi still asked: "If the hypostases were neither separated nor divided one from the other, then, therefore, the Father and the Holy Spirit are incarnated with the Word."[44]

Timothy's response to the Christology differentiates himself and the Eastern Church as Nestorian from the Eastern Chalcedonian, the Melkites, [45] and non-Chalcedonian, the Jacobites.[46] His argument is that "there are two separate points of origin for the divine and human natures of Christ …after the incarnation there is complete unity between the divine and human in him."[47] Although the long historical inheritance of fierce theological conflict between the Nestorian and the other rival churches; the Melkites and the Jacobites, regarding Christ's nature but Norris notes that Timothy was conciliatory toward the other churches. Norris writes:

> Timothy once (he) insisted that all three groups believed in one *ousia* (essence) and three *hypostases* (persons) in the Trinity. They [Melkite and Jacobites] confessed, in the same manner, our Saviour as true

---

[44] Hackenburg, "An Arabic-to-English Translation."

[45] The Melkites (faithful to the king, comes from the Syriac word (Melek) or Maximists (followers of Maximus) are the terms that "the Jacobites regularly referred to their Chalcedonian adversaries. Maximists because they accepted the Christology of the Greek theologian, Maximus the Confessor (c. 580-662) as definitive, and Melkites, or Royalists/Imperialists, because they accepted creedal formulae approved by the church council called by the Roman emperor Constantine IV, the ecumenical council, Constantinople III (681). For more information, seer Griffith S. H. (2011) "John of Damascus and the Church in Syria in the Umayyad Era: The Intellectual and Cultural Milieu of Orthodox Christians in the World of Islam," *Hugoye: Journ\al of Syriac Studies*, Vol. 11.2, 207-237, 218.

[46] Jacobites or Monophysites (the doctrine of one will in the person of Jesus,) are the terms that regularly referred to the non-Chalcedonian of Alexandria and Antioch by their Chalcedonians adversaries. They called Jacobites as followers of Jacob Albardai, or Baradseus, who was made bishop Edessa in 541.

[47] Beaumont, *Christology in Dialogue with Muslims*, 23.

God and true man. And not about the union itself is there quarrel or contest between us, but about the manner and kind of the union.[48]

Timothy's conciliatory approach was not limited to his rival Christians, but he also demonstrated a conciliatory attitude toward Muslims. Griffith states that in an introduction to apologetic letter-treatises written by Muslims and Christians in Arabic, Timothy describes the Muslims as "the new Jews."

Christ's Crucifixion

The caliph raised some questions about the cross of Jesus. The common questions most of Muslims ask are: Why do you worship the cross? If Christ is God, then Christians believe that God suffers and dies? Despite Timothy's fluency, persuasiveness, and expressiveness, his argumentations could not convince the caliph of the inevitability of the crucifixion and the puzzle of where God (the divine) was when Jesus died. This is because Muslims' reference to Christ's crucifixion is the Qur'an assertion: "They did not kill him, nor did they crucify him, but [another] He made a similitude him to them. And indeed, those who differ over it are in doubt about it." *Surah An-Nisa* [4:157]

The Trinity

In responding to the Trinity questions, Timothy used analogies and similes from nature, mysticism of numbers, logical common sense, philosophical thoughts, Biblical and the Qur'anic texts, as well as theological evidence to convince the caliph that Christians are worshiping One God, Triune in nature. Timothy's thesis is that "we can find, in nature, a threefold expression of the one and same reality."[49] Such as the sun is one with its light and heat, so God is one with his Word and his Spirit. The caliph asked to be shown from the Books that the Word and Spirit are eternal and not separated from God. Timothy turned to the biblical texts prove it. Once again Mahdi

---

[48] Norris, "Timothy I of Baghdad," 135.
[49] Samir "The Earliest Arab Apology," 71.

asked about the difference between the Son and the Spirit, and how is it that the son is not the Spirit and the Spirit is not the Son. Again Timothy turned to theological concepts: "[God] is not begotten, the second [the Son] is begotten, the third [the Spirit] proceed; and God consists of Father, Son, and Holy Spirit."

Timothy used analogies such as the apple, whose scent and whose taste are begotten and proceed from the whole apple. Timothy argued that:

> while scent and taste are mixed in a way that taste is not scent and the scent is not taste, and are not confused with each other, nor separated from each other, but are so to speak mixed together in a separate way, and separated from each other in a mixed way, by a process that is as amazing as it is incomprehensible. In the same way the uncircumscribed Father the Son is begotten and the Spirit proceeds in an uncircumscribed way.[50]

Timothy continued to demonstrate the Trinity from the Qur'an. He argued that the Qur'an conveys that Jesus is called the Word and the Spirit of God, interpreting the three letters at the beginning of some surahs as the Qur'an's mysterious way to teach the Christian Trinity. He also pointed out that the Qur'anic "plural form in connection with God, in the expression 'we sent,' 'we breathed,' 'we said,' etc."[51] These interpretations was not acceptable to the caliph as well as any Muslim. In the same way, Mahdi reinterpreted the Christian scriptures and prophecies and related them to Muhammad's prophethood. Such reinterpretation of other religion's scriptures was typically counterproductive to conversations and often ended up deeply offending and ultimately corroding the dialogue.[52]

---

[50] Mingana, *Apology of Timothy the Patriarch*, 26.
[51] Coakley and Sterk, "Early Medieval Christianity," 234.
[52] *ACU* (blog), "Timothy I and Al-Mahdi: The Great Debate," http://blogs.acu.edu/jks07b/files/2013/04/BIBH-674-Timothy-I.docx], 12.

Muhammad's Prophethood

A primary topic of the debate between Timothy and the caliph was Muhammad's prophethood. Mahdi employed biblical texts and prophecies reinterpreted to relate to Muhammad. He insisted that the original Books predict Muhammad's coming. Timothy retorted that he had never seen a single verse in the Gospel, in the (Books) of the Prophets, or in others, bearing witness to Muhammad, his works, or his name.[53]

Timothy's response to the question about what Christians say of Muhammad's prophecy was similar to the response of John of Damascus—that Muhammad had no witness to his prophetic authority since no prophet came before him had predicted his coming. He argued that Muhammad is not the last prophet as evidenced by the absence of the prophecies about him in the Gospel such as his name, his mother, and his people. He stated, "it is evident that there is no mention of [Muhammad] in it all, and that is the reason why I have not received a single testimony from the Gospel about him." He maintained, "as to us we have not accepted Muhammad because we have not a single testimony about him in our Books." In the Arabic edition read this way:

> Therefore, these verses and a number of others revealingly bear- witness to Jesus Christ; however, I have never seen absolutely one solitary verse in the Gospel, in the (Books) of the Prophets or in others, bearing witness to Muhammad, his works, or his name.[54]

Timothy's contended that the prophecies were fulfilled by Christ. Christ is the seal of the prophet, not Muhammad.

However, contrary to John of Damascus, who associated Islam (calling it Ishmaelite heresy) with the Arianism heresy and questioned Muhammad's authenticity as a prophet, Timothy viewed Muhammad

---

[53] Coakley and Sterk, "Early Medieval Christianity," 232.
[54] Hackenburg, "An Arabic-to-English Translation," 78.

as one who walked in the path of the prophets.[55] Furthermore, Timothy praises Mohammed for using the sword as a zeal for God. He stats, "who will not praise, honor, and exalt the one who not only fought for God in words but also showed his zeal for him in the sword?"[56] Timothy rescinded the allegation that the Books testify that Muhammad is the seal of the prophets, but he praised him as the one who walked on the path of the prophets, comparing him with Moses and Abraham.

Timothy argues that "who will not praise…the one God has praised him and, will not weave a crown of glory and majesty to the one whom God has glorified and exalted him?" This could be seen as a diplomatic approach to satisfy the caliph. However, Corrie Block argues that praising Muhammad "cannot be said to be mere flattery from the mouth of the Nestorian Patriarch." She maintains that "Timothy had a strong relationship with the Caliphate, and had no need for flattery to accomplish his ecclesiastical goals."[57]

Discussing Muhammad's prophethood, Block states that "Timothy certainly presses the caliph to prove Muhammad's prophethood, and outlines his community's objections." She maintains: "but that does not preclude that Timothy himself has not crossed the line of acceptance in spite of continuing concerns." However, Block argues it is clear that Timothy differentiated between the role of Muhammad as a prophet, and Jesus Christ, Word and Spirit of God.[58] Block states that

> When [Timothy] asked which religion is true, Timothy replied that the true religion, 'is the one whose laws and commandments are similar to God's doings in the creation', after which Timothy defined

---

[55] Bryan D. Rhodes, "John Damascene in context: An examination of 'the Heresy of the Ishmaelite' with special consideration given to the religious, political, and social contexts during the seventh and eighth century Arab Conquests" (master's thesis, Liberty Baptist Theological Seminary, 2009), 57, 58.

[56] Coakley and Sterk, "Early Medieval Christianity," 232.

[57] Corrie Block, *The Qur'an in Christian-Muslim Dialogue: Historical and Modern Interpretations,* (London, UK and New York, NY: Routledge, 2013), 148.

[58] Ibid, 149.

no religion, not even the Nestorian orthodoxy, which earned the admiration of the caliph.⁵⁹

Other Minor Issues

There were some other minor issues interwoven in the debate, such as, circumcision, prayer, and keeping the Jewish law. Mahdi as a devout Muslim who strives to implement Muhammad's life and keep his traditions was perplexed of why Christians did not follow Jesus? In his opinion Christians should follow Jesus. He asked: Why are Christians not circumcised like Jesus? If Jesus worshiped in the temple of Jerusalem, why do Christians turn to the east, not toward Jerusalem, in worship? However, he did not have any problem with the virgin birth without marriage, but it was hard for him to accept Mary's perpetual virginity notion—that the birth occurred without the virginity of Mary being defiled. Clint Hackenburg argues that "the crux of the issue was not whether circumcision or baptism was required or whether Jesus prayed in the direction of the east rather than the west, but that Jesus engaged in the human and earthly acts of circumcision, baptism, and prayer."⁶⁰ For him if Jesus engage in all these human matters then he is not God.

Conclusion

Timothy's apology is a Christian polemic in nature and conciliatory in tone towards Islam. There are many remarkable responses, some invaluable and sound. However, praising Muhammad for using the sword for God and employing the Qur'anic texts, the three letters proceed the Qur'anic surahs as mysterious symbols to the Trinitarian doctrine, and using the singular and plural speaking of God do not convince the caliph. The implicit agreement between the caliph and the patriarch that the Jews were to be despised and rejected was one of the weaknesses of Timothy's impressive apology.

---

⁵⁹ Ibid.
⁶⁰ Hackenburg, "An Arabic-to-English Translation," 28.

Timothy is a remarkable model of how Christians can boldly and wisely share what they believe without fear or intimidation. How could we get beyond the polemical approach toward conciliatory approaches to other religions just as this medieval theologian, philosopher, and missionary-minded model did? As Norris argues, "Timothy's public assessment of Muhammad is a grand place to start. This significant Christian missionary insisted that Islam was neither primarily a Christian heresy nor totally a devilish abomination."[61] Timothy constructed a remarkable model of Christian leadership for those concerned with making the Christian faith reasonable and appealing to Muslims, while avoiding an attack on the Islamic faith. As mentioned, dialogue too often turns to argumentation where there are already well-established disagreements. However, both Timothy and the caliph became more knowledgeable about the other religion than they had been prior to the conversation. Each gained a direct knowledge, or at least corrected his misunderstandings of the other. Nonetheless, the caliph ended the conversation by lamenting, "if only the patriarch accepted Muhammad..."[62]

This historical apology shows that something fruitful can emerge when Christians and Muslims engage each other in respectful dialogue.[63] This took place in an era of the Muslims' rule in Christian countries, where on the one hand Muslims called Christians *Hetariasts*, or *Associators*, because they thought Christians introduced an associate with God by declaring Christ is the Son of God and God. On the Other, Christians called Muslims heretics and Islam is the heresy of the Ishmaelite.[64]

---

[61] Norris, "Timothy I of Baghdad," 135.
[62] Irvin and Sunquist, *History of the World Christian Movement*, 287.
[63] *Sandalstraps' Sanctuary* (blog), "Timothy I and the Caliph Madhi," sandalstraps.blogspot.com/2008/06/timothy-i-and-caliph-madhi.html.
[64] Rhodes, "John Damascene in context," 60.

Chapter Four

Neighbor's Love: A Theological Understanding

Introduction

This project intersects with the inter-religious dialogue and intercultural understanding. It is not intended as inter-religious dialogue. Instead, the intended purpose is to encourage the Christian community to build person-to-person and family-to-family relationships. In the author's context, he believes that the collective history of the Muslim-Christian interfaith dialogue has not shown a real inter-religious dialogue. At best, it can be understood as a polemical debate: one side is right, the other side is wrong. We should nonetheless take initiative to build bridges between Christians and Muslims. By fostering trust and strong relationships and an atmosphere of confidence and understanding, everyone involved dares to ask hard questions. It would be easier to study the sacred texts in this setting of mutual engagement.

In this chapter, the author will discuss the theology that drives Christians and enables them to articulate their faith in God and relate to others: love of God, love of self, and love of neighbor. First, the chapter will discuss what prevents Arab Christians from reaching out and building relations with their Muslim neighbors. Second, we will discuss Wesley's theological understanding of prevenient grace/free-will and the faith of the servant as he was grappling with the possibility of redemptive grace beyond the church.[1] Finally, the research will discuss the mission and relationship.

Both Christian and Islam traditions have fostered fear of the other and ill will. Christians have viewed Islam as radical Christian heresy with Muhammad as an imposter. Muslim scholars and teachers portray Christians as the traditional adversaries of Islam. In fact, the average Muslim who sincerely follows regular teachings will find himself uncertain of his relationship with his non-Muslim neighbor—especially after the fundamentalist movements at the end of the twentieth century.[2] Does he consider himself to be "the nearest in affection to his Christian neighbor," as the Quran states in 5:82? Or must he heed the Quranic warning not to take Jews or Christians as "close allies or leaders" (Quran 5:51)? Is it the ideology that paints the other as an enemy and drives its followers to hatred? Certainly we must differentiate between Islam and those who ideologize it.[3]

The Quran distinguishes Christians and Jews from "those who associate others with Allah," (polytheists, or, *Mushrikin*) and identifies them as "the closest people to believers [Muslims]." Furthermore, it depicts as "the nearest in affection to the believers those who say, 'We are Christians.'"[4] However, it does warn believers not to take

---

[1] Kenneth J. Collins, "John Wesley's Engagement with Islam: Exploring the Soteriological Possibilities in light of a Diversity of Graces and Theological Frameworks," originally published in *The Path of Holiness, Perspectives in Wesleyan Thought* in Honor of Herbert B. McGonigle, edited by Joseph Cunningham (Lexington, KY: Emeth Press, 2014), 175–96.

[2] Muslim commands are addressed to males.

[3] *Merriam Webster*, s.v. "Ideologize," "to give an ideological character or interpretation to; especially: to change or interpret in relation to a sociopolitical ideology often seen as biased or limited," https://www.merriam-webster.com/dictionary/ideologize.

[4] Quran 5:82 says: "You will surely find the most intense of the people in animosity toward the believers [to be] the Jews and those who associate others with

Christians as "close allies or leaders" (Quran 5:51). On a different note, the Quran introduces the Christians as worshiping more than one god. Ernest Hamilton summarize the various qur'anic Christian forms of god this way.

> ..1) "Allah is the third of the three" (5: 73; 4: 171); 2) "Allah is the Messiah son of Mary" (5: 15; 72; 9: 31); 3) Jesus and Mary are "two gods beside Allah"; 4) "The Messiah is the son of Allah" (9: 30; 2: 116); In other words, [Christians] believed in the doctrines of the 'Sonship' of Jesus and the 'Holy Trinity' (The Quran refers to two versions of the Trinity; one, the Father the Son, and the Holy Ghost; the other, the Father, the Son, and Mary.[5]

Muslims believe that Jesus is a prophet sent by God to guide the children of Israel to worship him. They consider the miraculous conception and virgin birth of Jesus, the ascetic life he lived, as well as his other miracles as proof of his prophethood and the dignity accorded to him by God. The Quran asserts in many ways that Jesus is God's messenger and makes it clear that Jesus is the promised Messiah foretold in the Torah, the Spirit of God, and a prophet. Moreover, the Quran accords a position of great dignity to Jesus. Muhammad and Muslims make much of Jesus, his life, and his teachings. The Quran attributed a saying to Jesus in the cradle. According to Quran 3:46, Jesus spoke out of the cradle to defend his mother's reputation against the accusation of having a child out of wedlock.[6]

The Quran defines Islam as the religion that restores what was revealed to Abraham, Ishmael, Isaac and Jacob—Moses' and Jesus' religion.

Allah; and you will find the nearest of them in affection to the believers those who say, 'We are Christians.' That is because among them are priests and monks and because they are not arrogant." (Sahih International).

[5] Ernest Hamilton, "The Quranic dialogue with Jews and Christians," *Chicago Theological Seminary Register* 80, No. 3, (1990), 28.

[6] Muslims believe in the virgin birth of Jesus, however, sex outside marriage and having children outside of wedlock is *haram*, forbidden, and punishable by stoning according to the Islamic law.

> We have believed in Allah and what has been revealed to us and what has been revealed to Abraham and Ishmael and Isaac and Jacob and the descendants and what was given to Moses and Jesus and what was given to the prophets from their Lord. We make no distinction between any of them, and we are Muslims [in submission] to Him. Quran 2: 136.

How can we build on the fact that the Quran leaves the door open for a dialogue with Muslims? While there is common ground between the two religions, there are also many areas of divergence. When a strong, healthy relationship and an atmosphere of honesty and trust are promoted, our Muslim neighbors dare to ask questions about the authenticity of the Bible, the deity of Christ, the Trinity, and why God would have allowed his prophet to be crucified.

Christians on the other hand have to "…always be ready to make a defense to everyone who asks you to give an account for the hope that is in you, yet with gentleness and reverence." 1 Peter 3:15 In the same vein, Christians have a lot to learn from their Muslim neighbors. Does the Quran command violence, as some say? Or does it command peace? What is the source of the Quran? What is the meaning of Jihad in Islam? Does the Quran teach about radical Jihad; as radical Islamic groups claim?

Love God, Self, and Other

The theological approach to the Old Testament states that God loved Israel (Malachi 1:2-3) and has chosen them to be a people for himself. God delivered them from Egypt, the land of slavery. Because of that, Israel is obligated to love, serve, and obey the Lord. The Ten Commandments are divided into two tables. The first group of five commandments of the Decalogue addresses the relationship between humans and God. The second pertains to the Israelite and his neighbor.[7] In the New Testament Jesus summarizes the law of the Old

---

[7] Josiah Derby, "The Third Commandment," *Jewish Bible Quarterly* 21, (1993): 24-27. *Old Testament Abstracts.*

Testament into the two greatest commandments (Matthew 22:35–40, Mark 12:28–34):

> The foremost is, 'Hear, O Israel! The Lord our God is one Lord; and you shall love the Lord your God with all your heart, and with all your soul, and with all your mind, and with all your strength.' The second is this, 'You shall love your neighbor as yourself.'

The Hebrew scripture gives precedence to loving native Jews over loving resident aliens. "Do not seek revenge or bear a grudge against a fellow Israelite, but love your neighbor as yourself. I am the Lord." However, special attention was given to the strangers who sojourn with the Israelites from Egypt in the Pentateuch. There are assertions that they "must not mistreat or oppress foreigners" (Ex. 22:21), that they were to treat them as the native, loving them as themselves, for they had also been strangers in the land of Egypt (Leviticus 19:34). Jesus cited the first two commandments in the Law as the highest and greatest: love your God and love your neighbor (Matthew 22:35–40; Mark 12:28–34).

Love of neighbor is the summation of the entire Torah, as Rabbi Hillel states: "What is hateful to you, to your fellow don't do. That's the entirety of the Torah; everything else is elaboration."[8] This was his response to a Gentile who came to him saying, "convert me on the stipulation that you teach me the entire Torah while I am standing on one foot."[9]

Paul Knitter argues that the "historical Jesus,"

> Never intended to found a new religion that would take the place of the Torah and the temple, even though St. Paul in Romans 11 is ambiguous to say the least, still the early communities of Jesus-followers, as they moved away from Jerusalem and into the Greco-Roman empire, soon came to

---

[8] Bruce D. Chilton, Darrell L. Bock and Daniel M. Gurtner. Eds., *A Comparative Handbook to the Gospel of Mark: Comparisons with Pseudepigrapha, the Qumran Scrolls, and Rabbinic Literature, V 1 The New Testament Gospels in Their Judaic Contexts* (Leiden, Netherlands: Brill, 2010), 383.

[9] Mingana, *Apology of Timothy the Patriarch*.

consider themselves 'the New Israel,' the 'New Testament,' destined by God to carry on and to fulfill—which meant to absorb—the Old Testament and the old Covenant.[10]

The New Testament love of God and neighbor are rooted in Jewish traditions. Love is the very essence of Christianity and its DNA. Love is what makes Christians different.

We must also look at the question, "Who is my enemy?" Jesus taught, "You have heard that it was said, 'You shall love your neighbor and hate your enemy.' But I say to you, love your enemies and pray for those who persecute you." Matthew 5:43-44. Why did no one stop to ask Jesus, "Who is my enemy?" The simple answer is that everyone thinks she/he already knows her/his enemy. But do we, really?

Today there is a lot of confusion around this question. For Christians, and for many Muslims too, it is hard to know who is an enemy and who is a neighbor. In many remote areas in Egypt, peaceful Christians might find themselves under community attack, suddenly seen as an enemy by their neighbors, with the rumor that he/she is turning his/her house into a church. The prevalence of suicide attacks in the region also makes it difficult to distinguish friend from foe. Often it might be discovered that a neighbor standing in a church entrance is a suicide bomber loaded with an explosive belt or vest designed to kill as many Christians as possible, while calling them infidels.

So who is my enemy? Is it the person who declares war on me, who believes I am her enemy? Or is the real enemy the ideology that drives this person to paint the other as an enemy? For Christians, although we are commanded to "love our enemies and pray for those who persecute us," however we have to be aware of our enemy and not be deceived. Jesus said: "Behold, I send you out as sheep in the midst of wolves; so be shrewd as serpents and innocent as doves." Matthew 10:16. In the Beatitudes, Jesus blesses those who are

---

[10] Paul F. Knitter, "Islam and Christianity Sibling Rivalries and Sibling Possibilities," 59, No. 4 (December, 2009), 554-570, 558.

peacemakers (Matthew 5:9). The Lord asks us to love not only those who love us, because even sinners and tax collectors love those who love them. He asks us not to limit our love according to our human ability, but to expand its horizons and radiance so that we may allow God to love through us: A new commandment I give to you, that you love one another, even as I have loved you, that you also love one another." John 13:34. John 13:34.

J. Jeffery Tillman (quoting Don Browning) writes that psychotherapy studies show that the hate of self is a persistent human problem, and that self-love is the avenue that leads to the love of others.[11] Tillman continues by citing Gene Outka, who differentiates between altruism and agápē,. Outka defines altruism "as a normative concern for the well-being of others without a corresponding concern for one's own well-being."[12] He portrays agápē,. as "a mutuality that balances regard for self and others." Tillman argues that "under agápē, a Christian works unilaterally to establish relationships earmarked by intimate understanding and unity." He maintains, "although agape does not gauge its movements by the receipt of reciprocal response, it desires such a response from the other, even if such response is not forthcoming."[13]

This kind of love, agápē, that desires a reciprocal response, "best conforms to how God loves human beings. In that God loves all persons and finds each valuable, it makes no sense for God to demand that individuals demean themselves below the value that God places on them."[14] agápē, ἀγάπη, is a Greek term referring to the highest form of love. In the Christian understanding, as well as in secular ancient Greek, it is "agápē – properly, love which centers in moral preference. Emil Brunner defines it as "the unmotivated Love."[15] He

---

[11] J. Jeffery Tillman, "Sacrificial agape and group selection in contemporary American Christianity," *Zygon* 43 No. 3 (September, 2008) 541-556, 548.
[12] Tillman, "Sacrificial agape," 548.
[13] Tillman, "Sacrificial agape," 548, 549.
[14] Ibid.
[15] Emil Brunner, *Faith, Hope, and Love,* (Philadelphia, PA: The Westminster Press, 1956), 64.

argues that agápē is the kind of love that is not attracted by the value of the object of love. He maintains, "it is not being attracted or filled by the value of the beloved, but it is a 'going out to,' a giving not getting, of value. It is not comparable to a vacuum effect, a suction, but rather like a spring, gushing forth."[16]

Love, Hate, and Indifference

Hate is widely considered to be the opposite of love. But consider this. The well-known Holocaust survivor and Nobel Peace Prize winner Elie Wiesel once said: "The opposite of love is not hate, it's indifference."[17] Jesus said to his disciples: "If anyone comes to Me, and does not hate his own father and mother and wife and children and brothers and sisters, yes, and even his own life, he cannot be My disciple." Luke 14: 26. Does Jesus want his disciples to hate their own families? Of course not, Jesus uses the word "hate his .." to describe one's loving to someone else "less" in comparison with the others or prioritize someone's love over another. The *vocabulary.com* dictionary defines the word *indifference* as "the trait of lacking interest or enthusiasm in things. When you feel indifference for something, you neither like it nor dislike it."

In the parable of the Good Samaritan, the two people associated with the temple who passed the victim bleeding on the side of the road did not necessarily hate him; they were indifferent. They did not consider him as a neighbor who needed their help. They were preoccupied—whether because of a misinterpretation of the law or because of self-interest—while the Samaritan who was not associated with the temple and not a good practicing Jew showed his love and care. Through his loving action, he turned out to be a true neighbor.

---

[16] Ibid.
[17] Michael Denk (blog), "The opposite of love is not hate, it's indifference," *The Prodigal Father*. https://www.theprodigalfather.org/blog/the-opposite-of-love-is-not-hate-its-indifference/.

Love of God and Love of Neighbor

It is illogical if someone says, "I love God," and at the same time does not love his or her neighbors. 1 John 4: 20. Similarly, it is impossible to love God and hate self. As Stephen G. Post argues that "love is communion with God, self, and other(s). All attempts to consider neighbor-love independently of love for God and divine love for human beings are rejected in favor of an inclusive triadic or three-term reciprocity."[18] Karl Rahner put it this way: "Love of God and love of neighbor stand in a relationship of mutual conditioning. Love of neighbor not only a love that demanded by the love of God, an achievement flowing out from it; it is also in a certain sense its antecedent condition."[19] The Word made flesh reaches out to us. If Christians do not resolve the long history of conflict between themselves and Muslims, who else will do it?

Brunner argues that we live in three dimensions of time: the past, the future, and the present. We live in the past by memory and faith. We live in the future by expectation and hope. We live in the present by love. The present is the most problematic, as Brunner indicates. For Brunner, our relationship with Jesus Christ affects our past, future, and present.[20] Brunner argues that our preoccupation with our own past and our own future makes us "beings without" to others. He describes it as follows:

> An isolated existence is not human, because we are created, not to be isolated, self-sufficient individuals; we are created for fellowship. Therefore, we can be truly human only in communion with our fellow men. And that exactly what is lacking in us; we are never really present with our fellow men. We may be with them in the same room, but we are not really with them but only beside them. It is not about 'being with' but rather a 'being without.' We are shut in,

---

[18] Stephen G. Post, *A Theory of Agape: On the Meaning of Christian Love*, (Lewisburg, PA: Bucknell University Press, 1990), 11.

[19] Karl Rahner, *The Love of Jesus and the Love of Neighbor*, trans. Robert R. Barr (New York, NY: Crossroad, 1983), 71.

[20] Brunner, *Faith, Hope, and Love*, 13.

enclosed within ourselves, because we are 'preoccupied' with our own past and our own future. We are not present for them, not open and free toward them, because our hearts are possessed by our own anxieties, our own fears, and our own remorse.[21]

Brunner maintains that lack of presence is nothing other than lack of love.[22] To love someone is to be present for that person.

The Second Vatican Council, *Gaudium et Spes*, made it clear that making ourselves neighbors to every person without exception is an obligation, not an option.

> In our times a special obligation binds US to make ourselves the neighbor of every person without exception and of actively helping him when he comes across our path, whether he be an old person abandoned by all, a foreign laborer unjustly looked down upon, a refugee, a child born of an unlawful union and wrongly suffering for a sin he did not commit, or a hungry person who disturbs our conscience by recalling the voice of the Lord, 'As long as you did it for one of these the least of my brethren, you did it for me.' (Matt. 25:40)[23]

Neighbor-love is more than just fulfilling our neighbors' material needs. As Nicolas Berdyaev once wrote: "The true purpose and meaning of love is not to help our neighbors, do good works, cultivate virtues which elevate the soul, or attain perfection, but to reach the union of the souls, fellowship, and brotherhood."[24] This is nothing less than being present for others.

Prevenient Grace and Free Will

Another roadblock to Christians connecting with their Muslim neighbors is the fundamental Christian view that "the non-Christian

---

[21] Ibid, 72.
[22] Ibid, 72.
[23] Paul VI. Vatican II. Pastoral Constitution On the Church in The Modern World —*Gaudium et Spes*. 7 (Dec. 1965), https://www.ewtn.com/library/councils/v2modwor.htm.
[24] Post, *A Theory of Agape*, 27.

revelation is profoundly inadequate, limited and so cannot lead to an authentic saving knowledge of God." For them, "salvation is due to sacrificial crucifixion of Jesus Christ which occurred once and for all. There is no other way of salvation or similar to belief in Christ."[25]

In this section we will look at two Wesley doctrines in which Wesley tried to understand how the redemptive graces work beyond the church—namely prevenient grace and free-will. We will also focus on building relationships of love with Muslims as the soil in which the seed of the gospel can be planted.

John Wesley employed language similar to Calvin's about total human depravity, as well as about the universality of original sin, matched by universality and inclusiveness of prevenient grace. Wesley placed great importance on John 1:9, "The true light, which enlightened everyone, was coming into the world," and the Anglican *Thirty-Nine Articles* to support the doctrine of prevenient grace. Kenneth Collins states: "Wesley asserted that prevenient grace, based upon the salvific work of Jesus Christ, is applied to all people, Christians and non-Christians alike, through the ministration of Holy Spirit."[26]

According to Collins, Wesley identifies five benefits of prevenient grace, applied universally to humanity, which, together, mitigate some of the worst effects of the fall. First, "Wesley asserts that a basic knowledge of God … is revealed to all men and women as a result of the prevenient agency of the Holy Spirit."[27] He maintains that humanity has not been left without knowledge of God; we have at least some understanding of him.

Second, Collins argues that, although the human ability to comprehend the dictates of God's holy law was seriously affected by the fall, nevertheless, "Wesley affirms that after the fall God did not

---

[25] Francis O. Nwaiwu, *Inter-religious Dialogue in African Context*, (Rome, Italy: Pontificia Universitas Urbaniana, 1989) 19.
[26] Collins, "John Wesley's Engagement with Islam," 3.
[27] Ibid, 3.

leave men and women in this utterly dejected state, but inscribed, in some measure, a knowledge of this moral upon their hearts."[28]

Third, "Wesley reveals the ultimate origin of conscience is neither nature nor society, but God Almighty. 'It is undeniable, that he has fixed in man, in every man, his umpire conscience; an inward judge, which passes sentence both on his passions and actions, either approving or condemning them.'"[29] Wesley argues that, although conscience may seem to be natural because it is universal, it is in fact a supernatural gift of God.

Fourth, distinguishing himself from the Protestant Reformers on the topics of original sin and Calvin's doctrine of predestination, Wesley asserts "that there is a measure of free will supernaturally restored to every man, together with that supernatural light which 'enlightens every man that cometh into the world.'"[30] Wesley also distinguished himself from Jacob Arminius' teaching regarding free will "by asserting all good to the grace of God and by denying natural free-will and merit."[31] Finally, prevenient grace conveys a limited knowledge of God's attributes, understanding of the moral law, and the faculty of conscience to restrain human wickedness. "Wesley points out that God withdrew 'his restraining grace' from the obstinate and rebellious, from those who remained in idolatry."[32]

Although Wesley understood prevenient grace as a universal gift to humanity, he did not believe that it leads to salvation. It marks the beginning of salvation in the heart of humans. It is, as Collins argues, that grace which goes before the saving graces of justification and regeneration. Collins then asks in the light of Wesley's own theological constructs: "Are Muslims recipients of more than prevenient grace, even of those graces that make holy?" He put it in

---

[28] Ibid, 4.
[29] Ibid, 5.
[30] Ibid, 5.
[31] Ibid.
[32] Ibid.

another way, "may it rightly be claimed that Muslims are justified and born of God?"

Collins argues that Wesley "grappled with the question of the possibility of redemptive graces beyond the church (though not beyond the agency of the Holy Spirit) chiefly in terms of the servant metaphor (faith of a servant/faith of a child of God)."[33] Wesley "understood that salvific graces are communicated through a covenant relationship established by God."[34] Regarding Muslims, Wesley employs:

> The terms of the servant metaphor (faith of a servant/faith of a child of God) as well as with respect to his careful employment of the Apostle Peter's judgment 'Of a truth I perceive that God is no respecter of persons: But in every nation he that feareth him, and worketh righteousness, is accepted with him.'[35] (Acts. 10: 34-35).

Mission and Relationship

In general, Wesleyan theology stresses the relational nature of God's love: love that embraces and works with creatures, not against them, does good for them and does not harm them.[36] The Wesleyan theologian Thomas Jay Oord asserts: "Love requires relations with others. Love cannot be expressed in absolute isolation; love is inherently relational. Loving actions require sympathetic responses to others with whom the lover possesses relations. And love involves the promotion of well-being to those with whom the lover relates."[37]

In his essay "The Third Moment of Muslim Witness: John Wesley Had It Right," Terry C. Muck noted that the history of Muslim

---

[33] Ibid, 6.
[34] Ibid, 7.
[35] Ibid, 7.
[36] Bradford McCall, "Emergence Theory and Theology: A Wesleyan-relational Perspective," *Wesleyan Theological Journal* 44, No. 2 (2009), 190.
[37] Thomas Jay Oord, "Essential Kenosis: An Open and Relational Theory of Divine Power: Between Voluntary Divine Self-Limitation and Divine Limitation by Those External to God," *American Academy of Religion, Open and Relational Theologies unit*, San Diego, CA (November, 2007), 8.

and Judeo-Christian relationship is conflict and war. He argues that the bloody history between the three religions washed away the commands of the Torah to be hospitable to strangers, the Gospel command to love one's neighbor, including enemies, as well as the Muslim command to spread religion in peaceful ways, never by force. He states that the reason the Muslim world remains Muslim is Christians' failure of relationship with Muslims.[38]

Muck suggests that the mission to Muslims can be seen as comprising four moments: difference, identity, relationship, and witness.[39] Muck noted that the failure of the Christian efforts to reach out to Muslim cultures is primarily a failure with the third moment, relationship. Muck raises questions that shed light on why all the Christian efforts, including enormous resources, did not succeed in developing better relationships with Muslims. He argues, "Can we make a list of reasons without mentioning sin? Don't our pride and arrogance and triumphalist superiority have something to do with it?" He asks, "Can you really have a relationship of love with someone you consider inferior? It does not excuse us to point on Muslim and say that they seem to have similar feelings toward us."[40]

Muck argues that Wesley spoke passionately about the great stumbling block which prevents Muslims from gladly receiving the truth. Wesley argues that the West attempts to seduce Muslims with materialistic benefits of the gospel. Mock quotes Wesley's speculation:

> If we could change one thing, if we could change the relationships we have with the Islamic world, with Muslim countries, with individual Muslims, the Great Stumbling Block would be removed and 'the holy lives of the Christians will be an argument they will not know how to resist; seeing the Christians steadily and uniformly practice what is agreeable to the law written in their own hearts, their prejudices will

---

[38] Terry C. Muck, "The Third Moment of Muslim Witness: John Wesley Had It Right," A Theta Phi Lecture, *Asbury Journal* 61 No. 1 (2006), 83-95, 83.
[39] Ibid, 91.
[40] Ibid.

quickly die away, and they will gladly receive the truth as it is in Jesus."[41]

For Middle Eastern Christians and Muslims, relationships are far more critical because of the historical coexistence and because both communities share social, economic, cultural, and political conditions.

Muck proposes two of John Wesley's sermons—sermon 63, "the General Spread of the Gospel," and sermon 92, "On Zeal"—as containing solutions to the problem of poor relationships between Christians and Muslims. Muck states, "to truly love Muslims, to build lasting relationship with them so that we create the only soil in which the gospel of love can be planted, the soul of Christian love? Wesley says it is to have zealous humility, zealous patience, zealous kindness, zealous meekness."[42] Muck observes that these phrases sound odd. Could this be because we do not have a lot of practice in their use?

In her article, "The turn to the Other: Reflections on Contemporary Middle Eastern Theological Contributions to Christian-Muslim Dialogue," Sylvie Avakian argues that in order to rebuild and reconstruct one's own claims in relations to the other, there is a need to move beyond the modern notion of the critical approach. She proposes "scriptural reasoning" as a new approach to rebuilding a genuine turn to the other.[43] Scriptural reasoning is a communal dialogue where people from different faiths come together to perceive the scriptures as the source of reconciliation rather than a source of disagreement. Avakian puts it this way:

> Through scriptural reasoning, followers of different religious traditions–Christians, Muslims, and Jews– come to read their holy books together on a context of friendship, honesty, and hospitality, hence making theological and philosophical reasoning and argumentation and also a better understanding of one's own tradition possible, while endeavoring

[41] Ibid, 92.
[42] Ibid, 94.
[43] Sylvie Avakian, "The Turn to the Other: Reflections on Contemporary Middle Eastern Theological Contributions to Christian-Muslim Dialogue," *Theology Today,* 72 No. 1 (April, 2015) 77-83, 81.

>toward a genuine encounter with the Other. In such a context no one claims 'to know or possess the final meaning of the text under study.'[44]

In an environment of mutual critical consideration, negotiation of concepts, perceptions, and understanding, it would be easier to turn to the other. Avakian argues that Jesus himself turned to meet the Canaanite woman and the Samaritan woman. She maintains in such turns, Christians do not need to risk the truth or endanger the reality of Christ.

In her article "The Concept of Relationship as A Key to the Comparative Understanding of Christianity and Islam," Ida Glaser compares the idea of otherness and relationship in the interaction between the finite and infinite in both Christianity and Islam. She observes:

> Where the idea of relationship is weak, we may find that the infinite recedes so far from man as to be inaccessible and unknowable. It is towards this end of the scale that orthodox Islam lies—although by no means at its extreme. The Christian faith, on the other hand, lies somewhere in the middle. It is clear that God and man are other, but it also offers close relationship between them. The ideas of otherness and relationship are not considered mutually exclusive; and in this I suppose it to be unique. It is therefore a helpful basis on which to build a comparative understanding of other religions.[45]

Glaser goes on to discuss the Triune nature of God in Christianity: three persons in one, God from the eternity. She argues that God in Christianity is a God with certain characteristics, notably, holiness and love. Three persons in one God implies a unity in relationship. It

---

[44] Ibid.
[45] Ida Glaser, "The Concept of Relationship as a Key to the Comparative Understanding of Christianity and Islam." *Themelios, Vol 11* No. 2, 57-60, 57.

means that God in his nature is relational. It also implies that he relates to others. He communicates, loves, and acts in relationship to others.[46]

Glaser argues that holiness and love imply otherness as well as relationship. Holiness implies that the Trinity is set apart from others by its moral purity. It implies that holiness without active goodness, or righteousness, is not holiness, and goodness cannot be understood apart from relationship. Likewise, love makes no sense without an object. She asks, "If we remove the concept of relationship, what have we left? If we have the one, we cannot have the three. We can have the holiness, but not the love, and the moral dimension of holiness must be changed."[47]

Conclusion

Islam is a cohesive socio-religious-political system that is resistant to outside influence. Religion is an essential part of the public and private lives of people in the Middle East. It is rare that Middle Easterners come together without religion as a part of the dialogue. Muslims are skeptical and suspicious that any charitable and communal activities are the Christians' snare to convert Muslims. There are two Arabic words with historically negative connotations that illustrate this suspicion. The first, *tansir*, means to "Christianize" Muslims. *Tansir* is to compel Muslims to change their religion. The other is *tabshir*, "Evangelism," which is the Christian effort to convince, or witness to, non-Christians. Both words earned their bad reputations from the Western European colonial era, which connected imperialism and the missionary movement. All effort has to be made to build social relations between individuals, families, and communities. Social relations could build trust, the culture of accepting others, and sense of community.

To conclude, the author has contended in this chapter that there is both common ground and divergence between Islam and

---

[46] Ibid.
[47] Ibid.

Christianity. However, as Christians we have to follow our God and Jesus in the love of others. Building lasting relationships with Muslims, or anyone, is the only soil in which the seeds of the gospel of love can be planted. From the parable of the sower and the parable of the barren fig tree, Jesus taught that the soil in which we sow our seed is very important. To guarantee that the seed will produce good fruit, a farmer has to be careful about the kind of soil he intends to plant the seeds in. We can do everything right, but without good and lasting relationships, every effort to reach out to others will fail.

To approach the Christian theological understanding of loving the neighbor, the author looked at two of the Wesleyan theology doctrines: prevenient grace and free-will, and the faith of a servant. Additionally, the author proposed the idea of building a relationship of love with Muslims. Relationships build trust, and the bonds of trust can lead to love for one's neighbor as an affirmation to God's love. Open communication allows friends to "hear" each other and can provide insight into mutual value systems. Agápē love is doing what is the best of another regardless of the consequences. The hospitality to strangers is the first step to build relationship. Can there be a second step if the first step does not take place?

Wesley's understanding of the salvific work of Christ is similar to Calvin's in adapting the doctrine of total corruption of the human nature, which is the direct result of the fall. Wesley believed our innate corruption was eliminated only by death.[48] Contrary to Calvin, Wesley believed that because of Jesus' death, humanity gained free will as a result of prevenient grace, which became available to all people. God-given free will enables humanity to choose the salvation offered by God in Jesus Christ or to reject it.

Wesley employed two scriptures to support these doctrines. The first is based on John 1:9, "the true Light which lighteth every man was coming into the world," and supports the doctrine of the

---

[48] Mark K. Olson, "John Wesley's Doctrine of Sin Revisited," *Wesleyan Theological Journal* 47, No. 2 (Fall, 2012), 53-71.

prevenient grace. The second scripture, supporting the doctrine of "the faith of a servant," is based on the Apostle Peter's estimation in Acts 10:34-35: "I most certainly understand now that God is not one to show partiality, but in every nation the man who fears Him and does what is right is welcome to Him." From the beginning, God has revealed himself as a relational being to his creation. He made humans in his image. The doctrine of the Triune nature of God in Christianity implies relationship as well. Fundamentally, God's attributes such as holiness, goodness, and love cannot be understood apart from the relationship.

    The writer believes that Jonah is the perfect example of a person who disagrees with, or is maybe resistant to, God's commandment to love one's neighbors, particularly when the neighbors are considered to be oppressors, like the Assyrians. When Jonah heard God's calling to "go to Nineveh the great city and cry against it, for their wickedness has come up before God," (1:2) Jonah said straightforwardly to God, "God, look I will not do this for you this time." Jonah could not love people he considered unworthy of God's mercy. There are some of us who are in disagreement with God's commandments to love our neighbors as ourselves, but we do not have the courage to claim it. We use the same tactics that Jonah used, namely fleeing from God. Jonah's book deals with the question: did God have an intention to show his mercy to other people than Israel? Why send Jonah to them? Why did Jonah refuse to get to Nineveh? Why was Jonah angry when the Ninevites repented? How can we apply Jonah's story to our own situation?

    Jonah's prophecy and mission are unique among the prophetic writings of the Old Testament. The book focuses on a Gentile nation, a heathen people, rather than the people of Israel. The prophet refused his mission, ran away from God, then was greatly displeased and resented the outcome of his mission. Jonah was displeased by the Ninevites' repentance. He would have loved nothing more than to see them destroyed.

The book of Jonah articulates more about God's relationship with Jonah, and the relationship God wants Jonah to have with others, than it does about the behavior of the Ninevites. It is about God's dealing with resentment and bitterness against other people. Jonah was the object of God's discipline, and he became an example of how God's people should extend their grace and mercy outside their communities of faith. There are some of us who harbor resentment, bitterness, and a sense of superiority over people of other religions. Some have the perception that God is only here and not there. But God is.

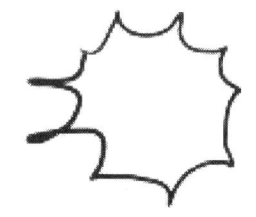

Chapter Five

Cognitive Minority: Can Make A Difference?

Introduction

The religious polarization in the Middle East has created a social gap between Middle Eastern communities in the USA as well. This project is not concerned with addressing the conflict between Christianity and Islam in the form of inter-religious dialogue, nor does this project have as a goal the conversion of Muslims to Christianity. Rather, it seeks to understand why Arab Christians have been marginalized in the late twentieth and twenty-first centuries. In his article "Christians in the Arab World: Minority Attitude and Citizenship," Tarek Mitri, a Lebanese professor and politician, argues that Christians became minorities in terms of the power they wielded in some regions of the Islamic world, even when they were outnumbered by Muslims. Mitri offers Syria up to the twelfth century as an example; he also contends that Arab Christians played a fundamental role in paving the way for the Arab renaissance, *Al-Nahda*, in the late nineteenth and early twentieth century. Major Christian figures played roles in the national liberations and modern Arab nationalist movement in Palestine, Iraq, Syria, Lebanon, and Egypt, despite their status as minorities in the region at that time in history.[1]

This chapter discusses why Arab Christians were influential under the Abbasid Caliphate, in general, and particularly in the eighth century and the late nineteenth and early twentieth centuries. How can Arab Christians go beyond what they have experienced as marginalized minorities? In other words, what can be seen by the majority culture as "normal"? Needless to say, other factors such as the rise of Islamist fundamentalist movements, lack of religious freedom, discrimination, and persecution against these minorities cannot be overlooked. This chapter will discuss and analyze the attitude of Arab Christians as minorities in their contexts and how they can move past the psychological traumas experienced in years past.

My hypothesis is that Arab Christians have lacked zeal for or interest in reaching out to their neighbors out of the intimidation inherent in being minorities, and thereby Arab Christians have ceased to seek and build up relationships with their neighbors and befriend them. Separation provides ignorance, and ignorance produces fear. My solution is to build an individual-to-individual or family-to-family social relationship based on "love of God" and "love of neighbor." I address this issue by recommending and creating a critical curriculum for transformation.

The antithesis of this claim suggests that, whether Arab Christians as non-Muslims do or do not enjoy full citizenship rights, they have proved that they are an indispensable part of their countries. They have played vital roles in the progress of Islamic culture. They have played a crucial role in the Arab Renaissance. They have been pioneers in thought, science, philosophy, and social advancement.

---

[1] Tarek Mitri, "Christians in the Arab World: Minority Attitude and Citizenship," *The Ecumenical Review*, V. 64, no. 1 (March 2012), 43-49.

"According to Fr. Samīr Khalīl Samīr,[2] the rise of the Abbasid dynasty gave rise to the participation of Arab Christians in the Arab Renaissance with the likes of Ḥunayn ibn Isḥāq and Qusṭā ibn Lūqā, among others."[3] My proposed solution is to build an individual-to-individual or family-to-family social relationship based on "love of God" and "love of neighbor." This researcher will address this issue in the next chapter by creating a critical educational curriculum for transformation.

This chapter will look at the crucial role Christians played in the nineteenth and twentieth centuries as well as the historical contributions Arab Christians made to Islamic culture in the eighth century. Additionally, this chapter will focus on the intersection of the sociology of knowledge and religion as presented by Peter Berger. More precisely, this project will explore the status of Arab Christians as a minority and the role they have played as a cognitive minority throughout history.

Arab-Christians: Role and Identity

Arab Christians played an instrumental role in national liberation movements in the Middle East, leading to the independence from the Ottoman rule and later the European powers in the late nineteenth and early twentieth century. They became a major agent of the Arab nationalist movement, which contributed to building progressive modernity in their countries. In his article "Christians in the Arab World: Beyond Role Syndrome," Assaad Elias Kattan discusses Arab Christians' role within Arab-Islamic civilizations. Kattan argues that Arab Christians not only contributed to the rise and blossoming of Islamic culture in the classical era, but also contributed

---

[2] Samir Khalil Samir is an Egyptian Jesuit priest, Islamic scholar, Semitologist, Orientalist, Syriacist and Catholic theologian. Based in Lebanon, he is a regular visiting professor of several academic institutions in Europe and the USA, https://en.wikipedia.org/wiki/Samir_Khalil_Samir.

[3] David D. Grafton, "Coptic-State Relations: Looking Back to Look Forward," in *The Cairo Journal of Theology* (2014): (5–24), 8.

significantly to the revival of Arabic science and literature in the late nineteenth and early twentieth centuries, which led to *al-Nahda* (renaissance) and modern Arab humanism, and paved the way for the rise of Arab Nationalism.[4]

What made Arab Christians active and influential in the late nineteenth and early twentieth century? How and why did Christians contribute significantly to the Arab world? In his article "The Political Marginalization of Arab Christians in the British Mandatory Period," Samuel J. McCann indicates why Arab Christians developed a nationalist sentiment vs religious sentiment, particularly in Palestine. First, he argues that the desire was to move away from religious identification as the basis for rights within the Ottoman millet system.[5] Second, Arab Christians "were exposed to Western ideas of nationalism" through contact with their Christian European counterparts and missionaries.[6] Third, the emergence of Zionism and Jewish immigration aroused Arab Christian resentment and opposition to Jewish immigrants. Finally, the religious connection to the holy land for both Muslims and Christians created nationalist sentiment.[7]

McCann observes that, "one of the central reasons for the influence of Christian Arabs on the early nationalist movement was their cooperation with Muslims. If Christians were going to have any influence on the Arab nationalist movement within Palestine this cooperation would be absolutely necessary." He maintains, "a census

---

[4] Assaad Elias Kattan, "Christians in the Arab World: Beyond Role Syndrome," *The Ecumenical Review* 64, no. 1 (March 2012): 50-53, 50.

[5] Millet System, *millet* is a Turkish word means religious community, or "people." The Ottoman Empire "identify people by their religious sect and separate them into millets, which constituted their collective ability to communicate, worship, and even govern their private lives along the guidelines of their own religion." [see McCann 3 and *Encyclopedia Britannica*]

[6] Samuel J. McCann, "The Political Marginalization of Arab Christians in the British Mandatory Period," *College of Arts & Science University of Oklahoma,* December 7, 2015, http://www.ou.edu/cas/hihistory/images/docs/13_McCann_-_Marginalization.pdf.

[7] Ibid.

taken of Mandate Palestine[8] in 1922 showed that Christians made up just under ten percent of the population. This demographic pressure alone forced Christians into cooperation with Arab Muslims."[9]

Another important reason Arab Christians were more influential than their Muslims peers was that Christians profited enormously from the contribution of Catholic mission schools first, followed by Protestant mission schools. Robert Brenton Betts makes an important observation. By the beginning of the nineteenth century, he points out that "the average Christian in the Arab East was far superior to his Muslim neighbor in terms of education and material well-being."[10] McCann noted that the Christians in Palestine were urbanized, which meant that their education level and commercial activity was higher than their Muslim counterparts who were more evenly dispersed among urban and rural areas.

Kattan adds an additional reason why Christians became more equipped to lead the Arabic renaissance, stating, "Christians are thought to have been both intellectually and psychologically better equipped than were Muslims to become the forerunners of the Arabic 'renaissance' because they had no reservations about adopting and propagating modern Western ideas and social models."[11] However, although the Arab nationalist (Arabism) movement held Islam in high regard, Christians viewed it as a secular political program.[12]

Arab Christians as minorities were caught between the rock and hard place. On one hand, they had to struggle with the majorities for national liberation from the Ottoman Empire, and later against the European powers. On the other, they faced difficult choices about

---

[8] Following the Allies' defeat of the Ottoman army in 1918, Britain and France assumed control over much of the former Ottoman Empire. The League of Nations entrusted Great Britain with the mission of administration and development of Palestine. Encyclopedia.com, s.v. "British Mandate."

[9] McCann, "Political Marginalization," 6.

[10] Robert Brenton Betts, *Christian in the Arab East: A Political Study*, (Athens, Greece: Lycabettus Press, 1975), 119, 120.

[11] Kattan, "Christians in the Arab World," 51.

[12] McCann, "Political Marginalization," 7.

external religious affiliation, social conditions, and political changes.[13] Mitri argues, "on the whole, Christians aspired to citizenship free from direct or indirect domination from abroad. While their fight for political and civil equality set them in opposition to the moribund Ottoman Empire, it united them with the Muslims in a national struggle for independence"[14]

For instance, after the First World War, the Egyptian politicians began their contact with the British occupation authority in Cairo. As a part of the national movement, the delegation was formed from Christians beside Muslim leaders. *The Morning Post* paper of 9 April 1919 described the Copts representative delegations this way;

> The Copts are more enthusiastic than the enthusiasts. They were among the foremost zealots in defending the nationalistic aims. The priests are urged love of nation from the pulpits in the mosques and in *al-Azhar*, and the *Ulama* and *Shaykes* spoke in the churches. One of the most arousing sights was the flag on which hung the Crescent and the Cross. The phenomenon is nothing but a politico-religious revolution.[15]

In the same manner, an Egyptian historian described the Copts during the same time period saying, "Copts were among the most ardent defenders of the national idea and the first victims for the cause of independence."[16]

Arab Christians were always under double psychological and moral pressure to prove that their existence was beneficial to their neighbors. Kattan calls this a "role ideology." He states:

> In order to survive, Arab Christians *should* prove to be profitable. Their existence in the Arab world depends on their ability to play an advantageous role for their

---

[13] Mitri, "Christians in the Arab World," 43.
[14] Ibid, 44.
[15] William Soliman Kilada, "Christian-Muslim Relations in Egypt," in *The Vatican, Islam, and the Middle East*, Kail C. Ellis, O. S. A ed. (Syracuse, NY: Syracuse University Press, 1987), 257.
[16] McCann, "Political Marginalization," 7.

> neighborhood. Along these Lines, Arab Christians would continuously feel impelled to convince their Muslims counterparts that their existence is beneficial, and thus socially and psychologically affordable.[17]

On the other hand, both the Ottomans and Muslims harbored suspicions that Christians had been collaborating with their European fellow believers.[18] Therefore, the onus was on Arab Christians not solely to prove to their neighbors but also to themselves that they were both beneficial and were also nationalists.

However, although Arabs were able to transfer from the prioritized religious millet system to a unified Arab identity, as McCann argues, there was still a gulf to be bridged between Arab Christians and Arab Muslims. The gulf began following the abolition of the Islamic caliphate in Istanbul in 1924 by the initiation of the Muslim Brotherhood as a religious-political organization in 1928 in Egypt. The Muslim Brotherhood instituted what was later called political Islam, and was one of the most important ideological events of the last century.

To indicate the backslide of the Copts' status in the late twentieth century, Antonie Wessels makes the following observation about Pope Shenuda III (1971-2012), who was the 117th Patriarch, and defender of Copts' rights, "who have the feeling during these times of rekindled Islamic fundamentalism that they have been relegated to second-class citizenship, not unlike the former dhimmi status of Christians in Islamic countries."[19] Mitri also observed the Christian anxiety by stating:

> Today, the anxiety of Christians in the Arab world and their friends is evident. It arises from the effects of their dwindling numbers, the economic and political failures of the national states in the face of rising Islamism. Preoccupation with survival affects

---

[17] Kattan, "Christians in the Arab World," 51.
[18] Antonie Wessels, *Arab and Christians? Christians in the Middle East*, (Kampen, Netherlands: Kok Pharos Publishing House, 1995), 137.
[19] McCann, "Political Marginalization," 9.

both their readings of history and their reflections on the future. Disappointments that are shared for the most part was their Muslims fellow-citizens cast a shadow over the vigorous debate and the previous promises about the presence, role, and vocation of Christian in the Arab world.[20]

What about the church's role of impacting Christians in that era? In Egypt, the church played a significant role, as we have noted earlier. Many religious leaders were involved in the nationalistic movement, especially in the revolution of 1919.

Since its beginning, the Evangelical Church of Egypt[21] in the mid-nineteenth century put equal emphasis on education and social services such as hospitals and medical services they instituted. Christian educational programs including Bible studies and the peasant literacy to read the Bible.[22] The author has completed a study on the impact of the American Mission Schools on Egyptian Education from 1854 to 1904. He writes:

> One of the characteristics that marked the Evangelical Church was the educational development of its members. The missionaries founded a center for culture and enlightenment that could radiate out from the local churches in every town and village. In some towns, the school was established prior to the church, but in all cases, the school was attached to the church. Charles Watson reported in 1898 that the education department of the Mission did a census of the enlightenment and literacy rate of the Protestant community. They found the rate of men who could read was higher than 50%, while the percentage was almost 20% among women. The government census

---

[20] Mitri, "Christians in the Arab World," 44.
[21] The Evangelical Church of Egypt (the Synod of the Nile) also known as the Coptic Evangelical Church, begun among the Coptic Orthodox by the American Presbyterians missionaries in 1854. Now it is the largest Protestant church in the Middle East.
[22] Betty Jane Bailey and J. Martin Bailey, *Who are the Christians in the Middle East* (Grand Rapids, MI: Eerdmans, 2003), 105.

> in the previous year said that the ratio in the state, including foreigners, was almost 12% among men, while the percentage among women did not exceed 1%.[23]

It is fair to say that there was a noteworthy change in all aspects of life when the church's mission was reaching out to the community and serving its needs.

The emphasis on social services in the Evangelical Church of Egypt led to the formation of the Coptic Evangelical Organization for Social Services (CEOSS) in the mid-twentieth century. The CEOSS was founded by a religious leader as an independent social organization affiliated with the church. It provides a variety of social services to develop local communities, serving the poor without regard to their religious affiliation. However, despite the frequent attempts to serve the local communities in cooperation with local congregations, these efforts remained separate from Christian grassroots. This is because the local church often adopts inwardly rather than externally focused teaching and ministry approaches.

Copts paid dearly for their participation in the June 30, 2013 revolution. Many of their victims were shot, and more than thirty Churches and many Christian social care homes all over Egypt were burned down or looted. However, it was worthwhile for Christians to protest against the Muslim Brotherhood president. For the first time in modern history (since the 1919 revolution), the Copts felt that they were full citizens, a part of the state of Egypt, and that they belonged to and defended their country. Christian participation in the recent parliament elections was full and effective.[24]

However, after the Arab Spring, there has been a radical change of state orientation toward the Copts. There is even a radical

---

[23] Ayad S. Attia, "The Impact of the American Mission Schools on Egyptian Education from the Mid-Nineteenth to the turn of Twentieth Century," (master's thesis, *The Evangelical Theological Seminary in Cairo,* 2013), 52.

[24] Interview with Dr. Andrea Zaki Stephanous, the President of the Protestant Community of Egypt, http://www.Youm7.com.

change of the orientation of the Egyptians grassroots which became more tolerant toward Christians. Thirty-six Christians, twelve of them as individuals, won in direct parliament free elections, which is a phenomenon that Egypt has not known since the 1924 elections. The success of the Copts in the folk districts where Christians do not constitute a majority is evidence of the changing mood of voters. They are renouncing sectarianism and choosing deputies regardless of religion.[25] No doubt the political and socio-cultural environment is changing, but it must be asked whether church teaching and ministry programs changed equally to match society?

The Theoretical from Interdisciplinary of Sociology and Religion

Again, what prevents Arab Christians from being more connected to Muslim neighbors today? How does the intersection of sociology and religion provide keen insights into research and the implementation of this project?

The Cognitive Minority

According to sociologist of religion, Peter Berger, the definition of a cognitive minority is "a group of people whose view of the world differs significantly from the one generally taken for granted in their society. Put differently, a cognitive minority is a group formed around a body of deviant 'knowledge.'" That knowledge could be a set of beliefs. "Knowledge," as used in the terms of sociology, he argues, refers "to what is taken to be or believed as a "knowledge."[26] In the case of minority this knowledge differs sharply with the majority in their society. Berger also uses the term "cognitive" as an adjective; instead of saying societies have bodies of knowledge, he uses

---

[25] Parliament of 2015 recorded the highest percentage of Copts in the parliamentary elections Youm7 News, https://www.youm7.com/story/2015/12

[26] Peter Berger, *A Rumor of Angels: Modern Society and the Rediscovery of the Supernatural* (Garden City, NY: Anchor Books, 1970), 7.

"cognitive structures."[27] According to Berger, humans are social beings. He argues that:

> Most of what we 'know' we have taken on the authority of others, and it is only as others continue to confirm this 'knowledge' that it continues to be plausible to us. It is such socially shared, socially taken-for-granted 'knowledge' that allows us to move with a measure of confidence through everyday life. Conversely, the plausibility of knowledge that is not socially shared, that is challenged by our fellow men, is imperiled, not just in our dealings with others, but much more importantly in our own minds.[28]

The cognitive minority can maintain its unpopular ideas or beliefs only if it has a strong community structure. If a religious minority in any society is devotedly religious and finds solace and support in their religiosity, aware of the nature of its distinctiveness, and it embodies the unique characteristics of the whole group, then that minority will not be engulfed in and transformed by the larger society.[29]

Berger argues that "the status of a cognitive minority is thus invariably an uncomfortable one– not necessarily because the majority is repressive or intolerant, but simply because it refuses to accept the minority's definition of reality as 'knowledge.' He maintains that, "at best, a minority viewpoint is forced to be defensive. At worst, it ceases to be plausible to anyone."[30] In other words, the cognitive minority depends on social support; once the group accepts and confirms the definition of the minority then "the knowledge" will continue to be plausible to them.

In her book, *Berger's Dual-Citizenship Approach to Religion*, Annette Jean Ahern argues that there is a fitting parallel between Berger's dual citizenship—sociology and religion—and Luther's doctrine of *Two Kingdoms*—the Kingdom of God, whose citizens are

---

[27] Ibid.
[28] Ibid, 8.
[29] Ronald J. Sider, *Rich Christians in an Age of Hunger: A Biblical Study* (Intervarsity Press: Ill, 1977), 192.
[30] Berger, *Rumor of Angels*, 8.

"all believers in Christ" and the kingdom of the world, whose inhabitants are not believers. Ahern maintains that it is possible to claim citizenship in the kingdom of God and contribute to the kingdom of the world without watering down the integrity of either kingdom.[31] She continues to assert that this is what helped Protestants embrace what Weber aptly called an "inner-worldly asceticism." Ahern wrote:

> [Protestants] have pursued their calling in the world rather than apart from it. The theological basis for Luther's emphasizes on serving God by being involved with the world was his belief that we are justified by faith and not by keeping the law, we are not saved through 'works.' 'For our arguments is' Paul wrote in his *Epistle to the Romans* that people are justified by faith quiet apart from any question of keeping the law.[32]

Jesus prayed to his disciples, that those who believe in him should not be absent from the world, but make the world better—to be salt and light to the world. "I do not ask You to take them out of the world, but to keep them from the evil one." John 17: 15.

According to Sider, "sociologists of knowledge have studied the relationship between ideas and the social conditions in which ideas arise. They have discovered that the plausibility of ideas depends on the social support they have."[33] Berger noted that a minority can maintain its defiant knowledge only if it has strong structure. In his book, *The Beginning of Wisdom: Reading Genesis*, Leon Kass approached the question of unity of the clan, the Israelites as a cognitive minority in Egypt, and the question of perpetuating the covenant on a quasi-political scale of the Israelite under the leadership of Joseph in Egypt. He wrote:

---

[31] Annette Jean Ahern, *Berger's Dual-Citizenship Approach to Religion, American University Studies Series*, 202. (New York, NY: Peter Lang, 1999), 118.
[32] Ibid..
[33] Sider, *Rich Christians*, 191.

Any new political group, no matter how well founded, faces the challenge of perpetuation, which is always endangered by threats of disintegration within and of assimilation without. Internally to overcome division and enmity and to provide unity and peace, and the danger of fratricide must yield at least to concord, if not to full brotherhood. Externally, ways must be found to prevent absorption into neighboring polities and cultures, both willing (by assimilation) and unwilling (by conquest). Perpetuation thus requires leadership that can promote internal cohesion and preserve attachment to the ways of the fathers, in the face not only of hostile enemies bent on your destruction or subjection but also—especially also— of welcoming neighbors whose blandishments and bounties make you forget who you are.[34]

Middle Eastern Christians were and still are endangered by threats of disintegration within and assimilation without.

In a previous chapter, we looked at the significant role Christians played in the eighth to eleventh centuries in Baghdad under the Abbasid Caliphate and the vital part intellectual Christians have played in translating philosophical, scientific, and substantial texts from Syriac as well from Greek into Arabic. At the same time, the Church of the East experienced significant, steady expansion under the leadership of Timothy I Patriarch of Baghdad, the Catholicos of the East Syrian Church, 780-823. By studying history, we can draw lessons and go forward with greater wisdom. We can learn from past mistakes. By studying the biography of Timothy I, and the contributions of the Christians to the Islamic culture during that era, we can learn individually and collectively.

Timothy I was destined to lead the Eastern Church at a precise time in the history of the East Syrian Church:

[A] time when Islam was in the freshness of its new faith and animated by the glory of those sweeping triumphs by which the

---

[34] Leon Kass, *The Beginning of Wisdom: Reading Genesis* (Chicago, IL: The University of Chicago Press, 2003), 510.

Most Holy...appeared to have attested the call to belief and the associated call to arms of his new prophet and messenger. With the final consolidation of the new faith and the necessary canonisation of its great document. had come also the dawn of a new civilisation, of which Mohammed himself had never dreamed, and the splendour of Bagdad, founded by Mahdi's predecessor, Mansur, had, to some extent, retrieved the age-long ruins of its neighbour, Babylon the Great.[35]

Why did Christians make this significant contribution to Islamic civilization in the Abbasid era (750-1258 A.D.)?

A quick glance at Timothy's biography shows that Christians were committed to their religious identity and participated fully in all aspects of life: theology, philosophy, and other relevant fields. Dale Irvin and Scott Sunquist argue that "Christians [in that era] were often more educated than their neighbors. Their numbers included a relatively high percentage who were merchants, administrators, scribes, accountants, physicians, and artisans." They maintain, "for Christians within the Islamic empire; such business activities earned them not only sizable fortunes but an important role as a source of wealth for the government that taxed them."[36] Also, Christians monopolized professions such as medicine, which brought with them social power and wealth. "Christian schools in Persia had been for more than a century centers of medical teaching. Medical knowledge and practices were handed down with great secrecy from teacher to student."[37]

In applying the theory of the cognitive minority to Christians under the Abbasids' rule, we notice that what made a long-lasting influence was that the Christians accepted the knowledge of being a minority—not necessarily of numbers at the time. They accepted their beliefs, which differed sharply from the majority Islamic knowledge

---

[35] Timothy I, *Apology for Christianity* (1928) pp.v-vii, 1-15, Woodbrooke Studies Christian Documents In Syriac, Arabic, and Garshuni, edited and translated with a critical apparatus,

[36] Irvin and Sunquist, *History of the World Christian Movement*, 278.

[37] Ibid..

and beliefs. As such, the knowledge of being a minority was plausible to them. Thence, they found much solace and support in their religiosity. Therefore, they were able to prosper and transform their society. The same might be said of Christians in the Middle East in the late nineteenth and early twentieth centuries.

According to the Egyptian sociologist, Rafik Habib, the Nasserite regime polarized the Coptic elite in the government by representing the state to the Church and the Copts (instead of representing the Copts themselves). This has directly affected the elite's role and influence and consequently created the gap between the Copts and government. Habib argues that the defeat of the war of June 1967 ended the Nasserite Arab nationalist' project[38] which left shadows on the common political project, and led to a defect in national identity and a sense of belonging. The most important aspect is that the 1970s (the Sadat era) were marked by many emerging Islamic movements, which were mixing between identity and religion. In other words, communal loyalties took primacy over national identity. Religion gave Muslims as well as Christians a sense of belonging and security.[39] Consequently, in the face of the rising religious sentiments, Christians felt threatened. It was during this time that Christians withdrew and isolated themselves.

Simultaneously, the church ministry approach became more internally focused rather than community focused. As a result, the knowledge of differing from the majority became implausible. For many, immigration was the easy solution (for those for whom immigration was possible). They left their countries carrying with them their knowledge and expressions of distress. Most of the minority who

---

[38] Gamal Abdel Nasser was the principal leader of the Egyptian revolution 1952 that led to the overthrow of the monarchy, then became the second president (1956–70). Nasser led sweeping reforms, which led to social and political movements named after him—Nasserism (socialism)—which were Arab nationalist political ideologies.

[39] Rafik Habib, *al-Gaama'a al-Kebtiah bein al-Andmag wa al Ena'azal*, (Cairo, El-Shrouk: 2005), 52.

were not able to afford to leave their contexts engulfed themselves in the larger society. Those who are active in religion engulfed themselves in the church. They imprisoned themselves in a psychological ghetto, and the idea of reaching out to their neighbors ceased to be plausible, which lessened their power and curtailed their influence.

At the same time, Islamic religious speech was ill-disposed, unfriendly, even hostile toward Christians. With the Islamists' call to implement Sharia, the Islamic law which considers Christians second-class citizens, or, at best, Dhimmis. The church, especially the Coptic, in some respects became a haven for the Copts. Intentionally or unintentionally, the church became a parallel community life. In an interview, *The American University in Cairo Press* researcher Magdi Guirguis argues that:

> During his patriarchy, Shenouda III [40][1971-2012] and his bishops tried to isolate the Coptic community from the larger society by providing everything, even music, theater, trips, youth camps, etc., in order to establish a parallel life, with the assumption of protecting the Coptic community from the rest of society, which had become more Islamist.[41]

Also, in the face of state intransigence, Christians in distress resort to the church instead of state institutions, which leads Islamists to accuse the church of attempting to be a state within a state. Guirguis argues that, "the only way the Coptic minority will protect itself is to stop isolating itself and build a strong relationship with the rest of the Egyptian society."[42] The church has to take its hands off the Copts.

Similarly, Mitri argues that it is not impossible to break the minority's fear cycle. He maintains that it would be difficult when that fear is created by "despotic regimes who overplay and instrumentalize fears. At the same time, they claim to protect them against fears which

---

[40] Shenouda III, (14 November 1971- 17 March 2012), the 117th Pope of the Coptic Church, known as the Church of Alexandria.

[41] Magdi Guirguis, "Coptic Researcher Reflects on the Late Pope Shenouda III," an interview, *The American University in Cairo Press*.

[42] Guirguis, "Coptic Researcher Reflects."

they themselves have provoked. They also instigate minority worries about their presumed future domination by the majority."[43] Or, a minority's fear can be heightened by their own leaders, who may exaggerate sentiments of insecurity in order to dominate them by pretending to protect them. However, Mitri observed that "the fears of Christians could be exorcised only through a nuanced analysis of Islamism, or through dialogue of informed elite."[44]

In concluding his article about the future of Christians of the Arab world, Mitri observed: "Christians can be neither apprehensive nor oblivious to the changing realities of their countries. They need to take 'the risk of existing' instead of being paralyzed by 'the fear of disappearing.'"[45] If this is true of Arab Christians in their Middle Eastern countries, the reality in the United States the situation is different. Under the rule of law, there is no reason for fear, fear has no place anymore, but there is a need for the risk of love.

Individuals coming to America from a Middle Eastern majority culture where everyone's "knowledge" is Islam, will soon discover what it means to belong to a cognitive minority when they express their Islamic beliefs in the United States. Fortunately, the situation is reversed. Arab Christians in the U.S. now feel they belong to the majority as Christians living in what considered to be a Christian society. Muslims in the U.S. know how it feels to be minority. Probably this is the time for Middle Eastern Christians to renounce self-centeredness and self-sufficiency, and reach out to their neighbors in the US, not as objects of proselytizing and converting, but rather to extend their love to them as fellow humans within similar cultural heritage.

There is an increasingly urgent need to consolidate a new approach to ministry. Education can be of course, one effective tool that brings about transformation. The next chapter will discuss in detail a transformational educational model that can help individuals to

---

[43] Ibid, 48.
[44] Ibid.
[45] Ibid, 49.

be socially changed through critical thinking biblically, theologically, and historically: a transformative biblical educational study that can help individuals give meaning to his/her experiences through a process of critical self-examination.

The sociologist Marshall Ganz employs the story of David defeating Goliath to discuss the ancient belief that "the strategic resourcefulness can overcome institutionalized resources."[46] He argues that a guileful, courageous young shepherd boy faced a giant veteran warrior, victor of many battles, while the military leaders cowered in fear. He raises a number of questions: "How have insurgents successfully challenged those with power over them? How can we challenge rules with power over us? How can we change powerful institutions that shape our very lives?"[47] Ganz observes that social scientists and historians differ among themselves in attributing the success of many social movements in the USA and around the word the last fifty years. He urges sociologists and leaders to focus on strategic leadership to bring about social change. Ganz states that the "strategy is how we turn what we have into what we need to get what we want."[48]

We must focus on the needs of the Arab community in Dayton. As foreigners, they face two barriers. First, the foreigner must acquire the necessary language skills to survive. Second, to thrive, he/she needs to overcome cultural barriers to better integrate into American society. The author arrived at the conviction that, with the help of the Mosaic Church board, we can address these pressing needs of internationals so that they may live successfully in their new society. The outcome would be great social interaction and building trust

---

[46] Marshall Ganz, "Why David Sometimes Wins: Strategic Capacity in Social Movements," 177-198 in Jeff Goodwin and James M. Jasper, eds. *Rethinking Social Movements: Structure, Meaning, and Emotion,* (Lanham, MD: Rowman & Littlefield, 2004), 178.

[47] Ibid.

[48] Ibid,.

between all who are involved based on sound biblical principles and truth.

Conclusion

The research explored the socio-political and religious impact of Christian minorities in their relationships with Islamic state majorities in the Middle East. Two examples from the past were offered: The Eastern Church in Iraq under the leadership of Patriarch Timothy of Baghdad in the eighth century and the impact of Arab Christians on the Arab nationalist movement which paved the way to *Al-Nahda* (the Arab cultural renaissance) that began in the late nineteenth and early twentieth centuries in Egypt. Both examples show that the historic Muslim/Christian relationship was strong when both groups were united in supporting the same political cause simultaneously social relationships improved. Common causes can unite diverse people.

In conclusion, when Arab Christians were open to cultural challenges and interacted with the challenges facing their societies, side by side with their Muslim peers, they played an active role in the progress of their countries throughout the ages. They also were afflicted by what hit their Muslims neighbors during the eras of decay. Christians played a vital role in the Arab Renaissance. They have been pioneers in thought, science, philosophy, and social advancement. They proved that they have always been part of their nations with its pains, hopes, ambitions, and aspirations.

Emphasis on Muslim/Christian common values can help overcome religious prejudice. These include monotheism, the sanctity of woman in the context of the family, and alms, and good works. Shared values can help build bridges rather than adding fire to already-burned bridges.

In the era of globalization, Arab-American Christians could play a crucial role in bridging the cultural gap. Their dual citizenship could help them to bridge the gap between their Muslim neighbors as well as the widening gap between the Islamic countries and the West.

Chapter Six

Why Arab Christians Stopped Socializing with Their Neighbors? Case Study

Research was conducted to analyze the impact of educational activities, critical thinking activities, self-reflection activities, and social activities. The project involved a focus group, recruited by the researcher, from the Arab Christian Bible Study community in Dayton, Ohio. Before and after two educational sessions—biblical, and sociological—the participants answer questionnaires, sit for interviews, and keep personal journals. The goal is that, at the end of the research, participants will have experienced a change in attitude toward the Other-Different and will be mobilized to reach out to them. This chapter will discuss the methodology used by the researcher to achieve project goals.

Hypothesis

The researcher claims that, historically, the social relationships between Arab Muslims and Christians were strong when both groups were united in supporting a political cause. Common causes can unite diverse people. This project argues theologically that building relationships of love with Muslims is the primary soil where the Gospel seed can be planted. The hypothesis is that Arab Christians were more influential when they were more open to cultural challenges and when they interacted with the challenges facing their societies. Side by side with their Muslim peers, Arab Christians played an active role in the progress of their countries throughout the ages.

Problems

After the rise of Islamic fundamentalism, Arab Christians as minorities in their contexts faced and are still facing psychological traumas experienced in years past. They encountered daunting emotional and psychological challenges that led to a sense of righteous indignation. Consequently, Arab Christians tend to allow fear to prevent them from interacting with their Muslim neighbors. Although this began in their native countries in the Middle East, Arab-American Christians carried their pain, trauma, and feelings of injustice on their shoulders to their new lands.

Purpose of the Study

The researcher sought primarily to explore when Arab Christians stopped interacting socially with their Muslim neighbors in the Middle East, and to identify the underlying reasons for this disconnect in hopes of providing insight and learning ways to connect. The research was designed and implemented to meet these project goals. The researcher recruited participants, facilitated two educational sessions, and conducted pre-and post-session questionnaires, interviews, and journals to acknowledge the problem in hopes that through this curriculum of critical thinking, the desired change might be achieved. The researcher then sought to interpret the data gathered from the questionnaires, interviews, and journals through a qualitative analysis to explore ways to connect Arab Christians with the Other-Different in their current contexts.

At the end of these three sessions, the researcher hope is that the study will help the participants affirm and declare the fact that God loves all people and wants us to reach out to the Other-Different out of his love. Consequently, the attendees will overcome the psychological gap, change their attitudes toward their Other-Different neighbor, and begin to build meaningful social relationships with them in greater Dayton, Ohio.

Data Collection

The research was designed for a two-session curriculum—biblical, historical, and sociological studies related to interaction with the Other-Different—delivered to the Arabic Bible Study group as the focus group who were born in the Middle East. Some were born Muslim and converted to Christianity, while most in the group were born in Christian families who later moved to the States. The project sought to interpret the data and evaluate the impact of the curriculum objectively through qualitative analysis based on pre-and post-questionnaires for each session, interviews, and self-reflections.

Bible Study Course Design

The researcher's purpose was to facilitate three sessions, recruit attendees, and develop educational material on the topics. Participants agreed to meet two times, every other week, to participate in worship, simplified studies, discussion, reflections, and individual questionnaires and interviews. The program was scheduled and the dates announced two weeks before the start date. The group was encouraged to actively participate in these sessions. The sessions were held in the church, and an average of sixteen attended both sessions.

On the first day of the program, the researcher presented the topic and the purpose of this project. The researcher provided each participant with pre-session questionnaires and brought to their attention the importance of searching their hearts and memories for feelings of hostility or antipathy toward their neighbors. The participants were provided with notepads and encouraged to write notes, reflections, and questions during the session. They were also encouraged to write their daily or weekly reflection on the topic and were instructed on the importance of this writing to help the researcher gauge their thoughts and opinions.

At the beginning of each session, the questions were based on three brief educational sessions as follows:

1. **Biblical: Loving One's Neighbor: An Obligation, Duty, or Option. The Good Samaritan in Luke 10: 25-37. (Study 1).**
2. **Sociological: Minorities Can Make a Difference. (Study 2)**
3. **Theological: Go and Do Likewise (Discussion)**

Research Questions

1. Is there a social gap between Arab Christians and Muslims here in the Dayton area?
2. If this has happened, what are the underlying reasons for the social gap between Christians and Muslims, in your opinion?
3. What is the responsibility of the church in helping to bridge this gap?
4. What kind of social activities can local churches develop to help Arab Christians and Muslims overcome the emotional and psychological barriers to connection?
5. How should Christians who live in nations with people of other faith backgrounds respond to the Other-Different?
6. Do Christians get opposition from fellow Muslims often?

Session One

Loving One's Neighbor:
An Obligation, Duty, or Option

The researcher presented the topic of research, the hypothesis, the problem, and the purpose of this study. Then the whole group took time for worship and prayer. Next, the Bible texts from Luke (10: 25-37), Lev (19: 33-34), and Deut. (10:17-19) were read in Arabic followed by a considerable time of meditation.

Introduction

Muslim-majority countries are entirely polarized by the ideological confrontation between Muslims and non-Muslims in several areas in the world. Confrontational approaches are often divisive and can drive away people of good will who long for peaceful and mature friendships. In such confrontational cultures, Christians experience prejudice, hatred, and discrimination. The researcher claims that Christians embrace righteous indignation on the one hand, and, on the other, they have been instilled with fear and ill will for Islamic cultures. As a result, Middle-Eastern Christians tend to allow fear to prevent them from interacting socially with their Muslim neighbors. As a result of being socially and politically marginalized, Middle-Eastern Christians developed psychological ghettos for themselves.

The *Standard Dictionary* defines *indignation* as "a feeling involving anger mingled with contempt or disgust, aroused by injustice, meanness."[1] Vocablary.com traces the word to its Latin root. It is composed of the prefix *in-* which means "not" and the root *dignus* which means "worthy." This means the anger is at something unfair or unjust. "A person who feels indignation is a little self-righteous and

---

[1] Vocablary.com, s.v. "Indignation,"

focused on not being treated the way he feels he should be."[2] In our case, this is the tendency to vindicate the negative feelings and not seek the goodness of those who we believe have thwarted us. With time, these feelings tend to turn into bitterness and blaming the Other-Different on one hand, and feelings of vindication of the self-turn into self-righteousness on the other.

What does ghetto mean? Vocablary.com defines *ghetto* as "a crowded, poor part of a city lived in by a specific ethnic group. The word is powerful, often associated with a rich cultural heritage or a sense of shame and a desire to escape." This definition points to ghettos formed through social forces in certain geographical places—often in walled ghettos for ethnic groups. However, "today, the word ghetto can also be used to describe non-geographic, but similarly cut off situations where one might feel stuck: 'the academic ghetto." Native Christians in some areas of the world find themselves in a similar situation.

Who is my neighbor?

At Jesus' time, the Pharisees, scribes, and experts of the law observed detailed rules and traditions that served as a hedge around the commandments (Matthew 23: 4). The neighbor was defined according to his or her position relative to this circle. The neighbor was someone who is similar to me. Jesus' parable challenged this definition of neighbor, and instead posited the neighbor in terms of needs-based mercy.[3] At the end of the parable, "the lawyer is forced to acknowledge publicly the correctness of Jesus' interpretation and is again exhorted to act with mercy as a neighbor toward those in need."[4]

---

[2] Vocablary.com, s.v. "Indignation,"
[3] John A. Szukalski, *Tormented in Hades: The Rich Man and Lazarus (Luke 16: 19-31 and Other Lucan Parables for persuading the Rich to Repentance* (Eugene, OR: Wipf and Stock Publisher, 2013), 102.
[4] Ibid.

Love, Hate, and Indifference

It is widely thought that hate is the opposite of love, but consider the thought of Holocaust survivor and winner of the Nobel Peace Prize Elie Wiesel, who, in 1986, said: "The opposite of love is not hate, it is indifference." Jesus said to his disciples, "If anyone comes to Me, and does not hate his own father and mother and wife and children and brothers and sisters, yes, and even his own life, he cannot be My disciple." Does Jesus want his disciples to hate their own families? Of course not. Jesus uses the word *hate* to describe "loving less" relative to their love for Jesus. Vocabulary.com defines *indifference* as "the trait of lacking interest or enthusiasm in things." [5] When you feel indifferent to something, you neither like nor dislike it.

In the Good Samaritan parable, the two persons associated with the Temple who passed the victim bleeding on the side of the road did not necessarily hate him, but arguably they were indifferent to him. They did not consider him to be a neighbor in need of their help; they were indifferent. They were preoccupied or self-interested, while the Samaritan who was not associated with the Temple and wasn't a nominal Jew, was self-giving and showed his love and care. "He saw... he felt compassion... he went..." Luke 10: 34. Through his loving action he turned out to be the real neighbor.

The Samaritan and Crossing the Psychological and Social Gap of Animosity in Luke 10: 25-37

> ➢ Jesus' Parable "the Good Samaritan" sets an example of someone who is willing to cross the psychological gap of animosity. The Samaritan in Jesus' parable demonstrates courage ("he came where [his enemy] was"), compassion ("he went to him and bandaged his wounds"), and love ("and he took care of him"). He was willing to rescue the man and sacrifice his own time, effort, and money.

---

[5] Cited from "Biblical Foundations" Chapter 2.

- ➤ The parable compels us, as it did its first-century audience, to break the religious, racial, and societal barriers toward the Other-Different. If that didn't happen in the early church—crossing religious, racial, and societal barriers—the Gospel wouldn't have reached us.
- ➤ The Samaritan in Jesus' parable created a "margin" in his life to help someone who, under normal circumstances, would have disdained him if they had met.
- ➤ To cross the psychological gap, we have to eliminate the distance between our neighbors and ourselves. Luke 10:30-31 made it clear that the priest avoided coming close to the injured man. He didn't even want to know his condition, despite that he could see the wounded man's tragedy from on top his donkey. "He passed by on the other side." The Levite, as well, "went over and looked at the man," (Luke 10:32b) "he too passed by on the other side."
- ➤ A first-century Jewish priest encountering a man lying half-dead on the road was under two commandment obligations. One which "forbids the priest to contract impurity by contact with a dead body, while the other requires the priest to show neighborly love to the wounded man."[6]

The *Mishana* obligated the priest to help, while the Samaritan was not obliged to avoid corpse impurity simply because he was not a priest.[7] In the oral Torah, *Mishana* obliges the priest to help the wounded man whether he was dead or alive. *Meth mitzvah* is the obligation to bury an unattended corpse, no matter who finds it.[8] This obligation takes precedence over the law that priests should not contract corpse-impurity.

---

[6] Bauckham, "Scrupulous Priest and the Good Samaritan," 379.
[7] Ibid.
[8] Michael Levi Rodkinson, Isaac Mayer Wise, and Godfrey Taubenhaus, *Babylonian Talmud: Original Text, Edited, Corrected, Formulated, and Translated into English*, V. vll. (Boston, MA: Talmud Society, 1918), 17.

Questionnaire Analysis

Fourteen participants in the first pre-session questionnaire represent five Middle Eastern countries: Egypt, Jordan, Iraq, Lebanon, and Palestine. The age range is twenty-two to eighty-two. Most of the attendees are over fifty. The length of time spent here in the States ranges between two years and thirty-six years. The reasons for immigration varied from seeking refugee status and seeking asylum, fleeing from political unrest, family reunification, to studying to pursue a better life.

In response to the question of rating the social participation between the Christian community and the majority neighbors in the countries of their birth and childhood, ten of the fourteen participants saw that there were strong relationships. Two answered there were no relations at all. Two responded that there were weak relations. It is interesting that answers differ even among participants from the same country or the same city. For instance, in the case of an Iraqi couple, the husband's evaluation was that there were no relations between Christians and Muslims at all in the city of his childhood, while the wife's assessment was that there were good relations.

Participant	Relation Between Christians/Muslim
None	2
Weak	2
Moderate	0
Strong	10

Social Relationship between Christian Community and Muslim Community in Participants' Countries

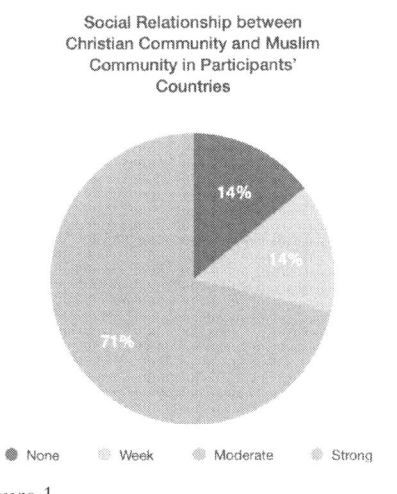

- None: 14%
- Week: 14%
- Moderate:
- Strong: 71%

figure 1
Social Relationship between Christian Community and Muslim Community in Participants' Countries

In response to the question about the family relationship with families from different religious backgrounds in their childhood, the responses were: 21 percent answered yes, there was and week, 29 percent answered yes, there was, and moderate, and 50 percent viewed it as strong.

Participant	Relations between
Week	3
Moderate	4
Strong	7

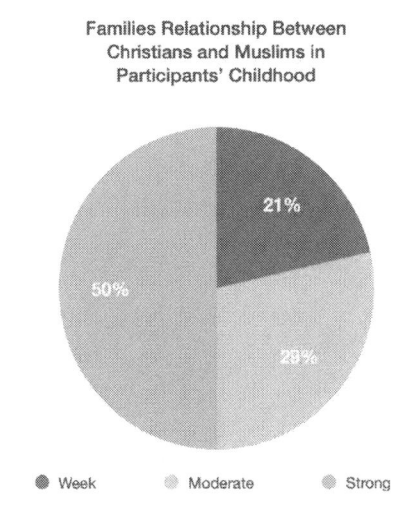

figure 2
Families Relationship Between Christians and Muslims in Participants' Childhood

Participants who had relationships with those of other religious backgrounds from their childhood and still keep in contact and occasionally meet were 57 percent. Those without contact with childhood friends from other backgrounds were 21 percent. And 14 percent do not remember.

Participant	Other-Relations
None	3
Few	9
Strong	2

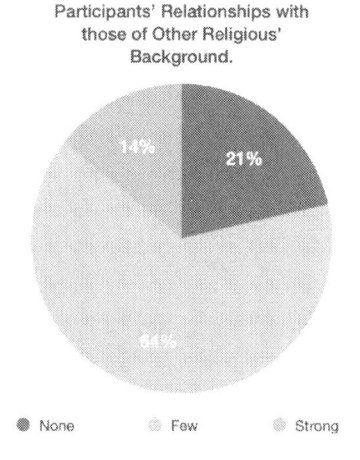

figure 3
Participants' Relationships with those of Other Religious' Background

In response to the overall relationship between Christians and Muslims here and now, compared to this same relationship as they remember it from their childhood, the responses show that 57 percent view it as being weaker than ever. Thirty-five percent of the attendees view it back then as moderate and the same as it is here and now. One attendee, who did not have any relationships with Muslims during his childhood, views it here and now as stronger than ever.

Participant	Relationship Comparison
Weaker than ever	8
Moderate/ same	5
Stronger than ever	1
Very strong than ever	0

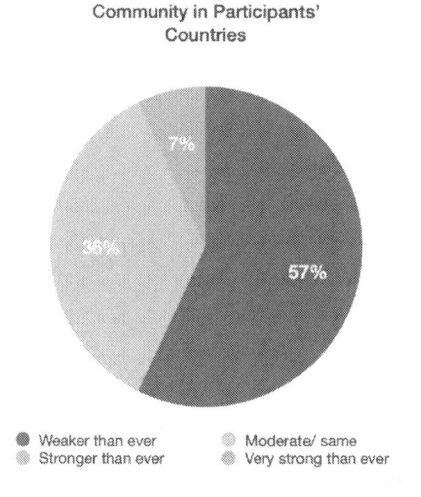

Social Relationship between Christian Community and Muslim Community in Participants' Countries

- Weaker than ever: 57%
- Moderate/ same: 36%
- Stronger than ever: 7%
- Very strong than ever: 0%

figure 4
Comparison Between Relationships with their Counterparts in their Childrenhood Then and Now

In response to a question about whether the participant has ever felt that he/she was treated the same as his/her Muslims colleagues in school, six participants (43 percent) responded that they never felt that way. Another six participants (43 percent) answered that they sometimes thought that they were treated like other Muslim colleagues, and two participants (14 percent) responded that they always thought they were treated like their Muslim colleagues.

Participant	Treated like Muslim
Never felt	6
Sometimes	2
Always	6
Don't call it	0

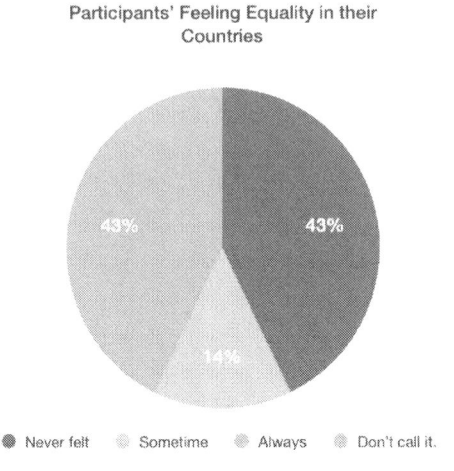

Participants' Feeling Equality in their Countries

43% / 43% / 14%

Never felt · Sometime · Always · Don't call it.

figure 5
Participants' Feeling Equality in their Countries

In response to the question if the participant ever felt bitterness/resentment toward Muslim neighbors back in their childhood. Six of the participants felt this way sometimes. Seven of them they viewed themselves as they did not and one, did not have it but overall he feels some injustice.

Participant	Resentment toward Muslims
Never felt resentment	7
Felt injustice	1
Felt resentment	6
Don't call it	0

Participants' Resentment Toward Muslim Neighbors Back in their Childhood.

43% / 43% / 14%

Never felt · Sometime · Always · Don't call it.

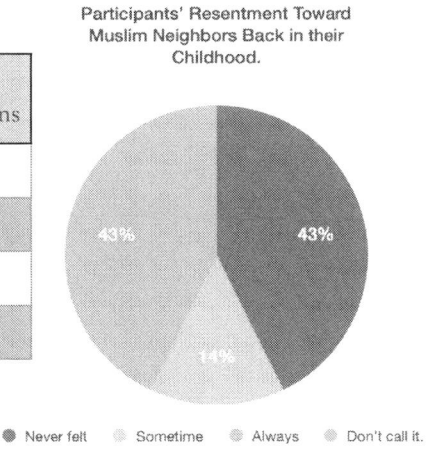

figure 6
Participants' Resentment Toward Muslim Neighbors Back in their Childhood.

In response to a question, if you would nominate one or more neighborhood activities that you could do to connect with your neighbors in the future, the participants did not really provide activities. Some of them believe that Muslim communities are closed, not open to the other religions, and that they deny other opinions. One participant reasoned that the reason Muslims do not socialize with Christians is because they feel guilty about what they did to us, Christians in Iraq. However, the participants share significant stories about the interaction with their neighbors. Later on in this chapter, the researcher will share these stories through the individual interviews.

General Notes Generated from The Results
- Most of the participants have been, and still, live away from their countries for a long time. Some of them are still connected, and some are not. Many of them have childhood memories of family relationships with their Muslim neighbors.
- Some have painful memories of what the fundamentalists did to them or their relatives who still live there. The participants did not suggest social activities to reach out to their neighbors, showing that they are not serious about changing. In my estimation, the reason might be because they do not know many of their Muslim Neighbors.
- The qualitative research method results showed marginal change due to subsequent challenges when subjects returned to their respective communities.
- The question that this research raises is if the participants were still living in a predominantly Muslim country would the results be the same? What would be the participants' feelings, their extent of openness, and the expected change? The matter needs further research.

Session Two
Cognitive Minority

Introduction

This session discussed and analyzed the attitude of Arab Christians as minorities in their contexts, and how they may move past psychological traumas experienced in years past. In this session, the researcher presented the definition of *cognitive minority*, as well as the historical impact of Arab Christians in their countries in the nineteenth and twentieth centuries. He set forth the impact of the American Mission in social and political life in Egypt as an example. The question was asked, "How can Arab Christians go beyond what they have experienced as marginalized minorities?"

The research hypothesis is that Arab Christians have lacked zeal for or interest in reaching out to their neighbors due to the intimidation inherent in being minorities, and, therefore, Arab Christians have ceased building relationships with their neighbors. Separation creates ignorance, and ignorance produces fear. My solution is to build an individual-to-individual or family-to-family social relationship based on the "love of God" and "love of neighbor."

Minorities Can Make a Difference
The Power of Small Things

Little things can have a huge impact—harmful or beneficial. A little sin, for instance, can be lethal. A big city or a vast forest can be set on fire by a tiny flame. Jesus taught that the grain of mustard is a tiny seed, but when full-grown it becomes a big tree with significant results. By the same token, salt is small and inexpensive. However its value and impact far outweigh its size. A small quantity of salt has a positive effect on food. Likewise, Christians can impact their societies. Jesus calls us to be the salt and the light of the world. Light can function as a landmark and give a reference point of direction for those who are lost in the dark. Paul calls the believers of Philippi to shine as lights among the people of the world.

In the realm of sociology, the same logic holds true. The theologian and sociologist Peter Berger defined a *cognitive minority* as a "group of people whose view of the world differs significantly from the one generally taken for granted in their society."[9] The cognitive minority holds a set of beliefs that differ sharply from the majority knowledge, ideas, beliefs, or views in their society. While social psychologists such as Asch argue that majorities have a large influence on minorities, Serge Moscovici and Lange (working in 1976) showed that the reverse influence is also possible. Minorities can be a source of social change, they progressing the views of the majority if they remain consistent in their responses and steadfast in their positions.[10] The minority is more influential when it appears confident and able to make personal sacrifices.

Arab Christians played an instrumental role in national liberation movements in the Middle East leading to independence from the Ottoman rule and, later, European powers in the late nineteenth and twentieth centuries. The researcher presented the impact of the American Mission in Egypt as an example. Since its beginning in the mid-nineteenth century, in addition to the spiritual services, the mission put an equal emphasis on education and social services like hospitals and medical services. These institutions offered services to all Christians and Muslims. As a result, this movement:

> … culminated in the contributions of Christians in the political life at the beginning of the twentieth century, which is considered the golden era of Egyptian liberalism. These contributions were represented in the leadership of Boutros-Ghali Pasha as the Ministry of Foreign Affairs for decades before becoming the first Coptic prime minister of Egypt in

---

[9] Cited from "Theoretical Foundations" Chapter 5.
[10] Paul M. H. Ashford, "Social Psychological Dimensions in Environmental Response" (Guildford, UK: University of Surrey, 1994), 44, 45.

1908. In this period many of the prominent Copts like Wassīf Wīssā, Akḥnoūkḥ Fānoūs, and Makram cEbeīd participated in the national movement, such as the establishment of political parties, the establishment of the first university and also played a key role in the 1919 revolution and the establishment of the Wafd Party.[11]

This was an inexorable shift in the Christian community's status in the early twentieth century. From being dealt with for centuries as *dhimūs*, to participating in national leadership positions, the shift was one fruit of the missionary movement in serving society. When Christians are open to reaching their communities, the outcome is for the common good.

Questionnaire Analysis

- o In response to the question about whether Christians were marginalized or not in the participant country, there was almost a complete consensus that Christians are marginalized in their ME countries.
- o There was a consensus that minorities could influence majority beliefs in any given society. It is biblical and sociological, but when it comes to their communities, there was division about the possibility that their Christian minority could influence the Muslim majority behaviors. Some believe that it is almost impossible that minorities could change the Muslim majority. They believe the Muslim communities are closed, not open to the other religions and deny any other opinions.
- o In response to the question, "What does it feel like as a minority in your own country?" we have to keep in mind that the migrants left their countries for different reasons. Most sought a better life or to escape persecution. Others came to pursue a higher degree or to catch up with their families here. It makes sense that most feel unappreciated.

---

[11] Attia, "The Impact of the American Mission," 52.

- In response to the question, "Have you ever seen any Christian influence in your society politically, socially and religiously?" one participant gave an example of the effective role of church in society. His maternal grandfather founded a church in a remote village in Upper Egypt in the 1930s and built a school for boys and girls affiliated with the church. At a time when society was not accepting of girls' education, that school made a huge difference.
- The responses given to the question about whether they have seen any Christian influence in their society politically, socially, or religiously were not specific. There were general comments such as, we should accept Muslim neighbors, love them, and show them Christian love. One example was about Mother Theresa, who is not Arabic nor did she minister in Arab countries. However, there were significant stories told about the impact of Christian in participants' home countries before the rise of the Islamic fundamentalist movement.
- Although many of the participants had significant stories with their neighbor Muslims here and there, they tended to be temporary relations that did not evolve into meaningful long-term relationships.

Individual Interviews
- To answer the question of when the social disintegration between Christians and Muslims happened in the Middle East, participants pointed to the fundamentalists.
- In Egypt, Nasser's socialist reforms, such as the industries nationalization policies and the agrarian reforms adversely affected many Christians families. Nasser also, marginalized the Christians in the political and administrative system. However, the relationship between Muslims and Christians was pretty good.

- The significant change in the attitude toward Christians began when Sadat assumed power in 1970 after Nasser's death. After taking office, Sadat began his rule by a coalition with Islamic political-religious groups—radicals such as the Muslim Brotherhood—against his political opponents.
- Sadat was the first to introduce the clause: Sharia law is the principal source of legislation into the Egyptian constitution in 1971. He used to say: I am a Muslim president to an Islamic state," with all its negative implications. The clashes between Muslims and Christians started as early as 1972. That era ended in 1981 with Sadat's assassination at the hands of the same Islamist groups whom he allied. His policies have torn the social fabric and left a devastating effect on Egyptian society, particularly Christians.
- As for the post-Sadat era, a golden opportunity introduced itself to Hosni Mubarak - who was thrown to the presidency in 1981 by the events following Sadat's assassination- to bring the desired political and societal change. However, to prolong his rule, Mubarak used the Muslim Brotherhood in the political game on the one hand. On the other, he used the Muslim Brotherhood to intimidated Christians by the Islamist's rule. Mubarak regime ended in a resounding fall in 2011. Muslim Brotherhood's rule was a nightmare for Christians. Fortunately, it did not last more than a year. Muslim Brotherhood was overthrown in 2013 by a grassroots revolution in which Christians actively participated. After 2013, there was a slight breakthrough in the situation of Christians politically and socially, but Christians still have to make more effort to get out of political and social isolation.
- In Iraq disintegration happened after Saddam Hussein took power. Like Nasser, Saddam Hussein was a socialist Arab nationalist in his political ideology. He was a product of the Arab nationalist movement. Iraqi participants in this study saw

the beginning of social disconnection between Christians and Muslims as the year following 2003, after the invasion of Iraq and Saddam Hussein's fall from power. Saddam's removal upset the balance of power in the region and unleashed Islamist extremists.

- The Egyptians and Iraqis mentioned that in both countries the beginning of the social disintegrations was the use of mosques as platforms for anti-Christian rhetoric, calling Christians infidels, which ignited and fueled sectarian hatred. One of the Iraqi ladies mentioned that women were forced to wear the hijab and loose-fitting clothing that meets the Islamic dress code. If they refused, they faced the threat of death. Violence broke out in Iraq against Christians: abduction, torture, murder, assassination of clerics, and bombing of churches. Christians were displaced from their houses and their properties seized by government gangs. The number of Christians has declined, and Christianity in Iraq faces extinction after most Christians fled.
- Lebanon is the most religiously diverse state in the Middle East countries. It is comprised of a mix of Christians, Muslims, and Druze. These religious sects coexisted peacefully until a sectarian war erupted on April 13, 1975, ended by the Taif Agreement in 1989. In that civil war, hundreds of thousands of people were killed both sides. During this civil war, Beirut was divided into two regions: the Eastern province was mostly Christian, and the Western was was mixed with an Islamic majority. That is why many participants did not have relationships with Muslims back in their countries.

Some of the Stories Shared about Socializing with Muslims

Stories from Egypt

- One participant from Egypt managed to have relations with his fellow Muslim workers over the years before coming to the States. He shared about a young man at his work. He encouraged him financially to complete his studies, which helped him to be promoted in his career. For some reason after the participant's emigration, this young man joined one of the Islamic extremist groups however he is still a matter of friendship.
- Another participant shared that a few years ago, he and his family met a group of Egyptian Muslim women journalists who came to a Cincinnati Enquirer training program. They knew about them from their program supervisor, who was one of the family's church members. The family arranged for the women to spend Thanksgiving celebration with them. Then, they took them on a tour of the city and helped them buy what they needed. The family overwhelmed the women with the love of Christ. That visit has left an undeniable impact on the women's lives. They were so appreciative and thankful. The family hoped they would stay connected after the women returned to Egypt, but unfortunately that did not happen.
- Another story, years ago, his brother met an Egyptian Muslim doctor who worked as the head of allergies and immunology at Al-Azhar University in Cairo. Al-Azhar is an Islamic University that does not admit Christians as students or staff. That doctor came to attend a training program at Cincinnati University. The participant's brother invited him to visit his center for the treatment of allergies and immunology. He gave him all the help and advice he needed during his visit. When the Egyptian doctor left the States, that brother gave him a specialized

medical apparatus as a gift of a good will. That man returned to his country, telling stories about what a Christian doctor did for him despite the differences in faith.

Stories from Lebanon

- o A participant who grew up in Lebanon shared this: In Lebanon, villages are either 100 percent Muslims or 100 percent Christians. Hence, when he was growing up he never had interaction with Muslims. On the other hand, things have changed now that he lives in the States. As a professor at the University of Dayton, he has many Saudi and other Muslim students from Arab countries. "I interact with them at the level of student-professor," he said. The professor noticed that many Saudi females prefer to register for their class with him despite the fact that there are two Muslim professors in the same department. One time, he asked a group of them why that was. Their replies shocked him. "We prefer to work with you," they said. "You are Christian, but we feel comfortable around you." They said being Christian was the main reason he treated them with respect.

Testimonies from Iraq
Introduction

This researcher dedicated a whole chapter to studying the historical impact of Iraqi Christians on the Islamic civilization of the eightieth century. It was interesting to see the sharp change in relations from that time to the twenty-first century through the gloomy testimonies from the study participants. Also, the researcher dedicated part of the theoretical chapter to discuss the impact of the Arab Christians nationalist on the Arab Renaissance. So he included these two testimonies to show the sharp contrast between now and then. The testimonies explained when and why the disintegration between the Muslims and Christians happened in Iraq. The research kept the names anonymous, and he obtained their consent to publish.[12]

First Testimony
- I was born and raised in the city of Mosul and in a neighborhood inhabited by Christians. My primary education was in a Christian school. However, we were oppressed by Muslim children because the families were inciting their children against us. Islam in Mosul is religiously intolerant and many people detest Christians. The situation in Baghdad is different; the religious commitment is less because diversity is higher in middle school, the distinction between Christians and Muslims has eased. However, there was still some discrimination from some teachers.
- By seizing power in 1968, the Ba'ath[13] party as a secular organization consolidated its power by banning all religious sectarian, tribal, racial, and regional "factions." The party succeeded in fostering tolerance and peaceful sectarian conflict between Shiites and Sunnis despite the influence of Iran's Islamic Revolution in 1979.
- As a university professor, we lived in a residential complex of professors from 1988 to 2003. Our relationship was very good with our Sunni and Shiite Muslim neighbors. That is because the residents of the compound were university professors, doctors, and engineers. Also, under Saddam's rule, no one dared to be sectarian. However, after 2003, sectarianism emerged on the surface from some families. We still have good contacts with many of these families in Iraq and abroad.

---

[12] This is the author's interpolation. Original testimony is written in Arabic.
[13] Ba'ath, is an Arabic word meaning, "renaissance," "awakening," or "resurrection." The Ba'ath party is a mix between Arab nationalist, pan-Arabism, socialist, and revolutionary believed in the unity and freedom of the Arab nations within its homeland. The party was founded first by Michel Aflaq (Christian) in Syria, 1947, and seized power in 1968 in Iraq.

- After the US invasion in 2003, once again the abhorrent sectarianism that divided Iraq's fabric between Sunnis and Shi'ites emerged, and sectarian violence has escalated. The victims mostly were the minority, especially, the marginalized Christians where the churches were blown up, Christians were targeted to be killed, and their properties were seized.
- As a family, we went through harsh times. We were exposed to death many times. For instance, in 2007, I was subjected to a kidnapping attempt by Shia militia groups. The Lord saved me with a divine miracle. It was that time we decided to leave the country because the voice of the Lord was clear in Matthew 10: 14: "Whoever does not receive you, nor heed your words, as you go out of that house or that city, shake the dust off your feet." So in mid-2007, we left the country and all our housing and jobs to Beirut, Lebanon, seeking asylum in the United States.
- After we left in 2010, a Shiite criminal gang broke into my sister's house. She and her elderly husband were slaughtered. The Islamic gang carved the cross on their bodies and carved Islamic slogans on the walls, "There is no god but Allah. Allahu Akbar." But they did not steal the house.
- The people of Mosul generally cooperated with those gangs called ISIS to identify the property of Christians. They wrote the Arabic letter ن as a sign that the property was owned by Christians, so ISIS would rob them. Christians who remained in Mosul faced three choices: convert to Islam, pay tribute to be protected by Islam, or face the sword. These barbaric gangs destroyed all the historic churches and monasteries of Mosul, which have profound historical archeological treasures. Also, as soon as ISIS captured Mosul, they banned selling food and groceries to Christians. In Baghdad, all liquor sellers were killed, and their shops have been blown up.

- Regarding our relationship with our Muslim neighbors here in the States, all I can say is that there is a certain coldness in the relationship between Muslims and Christians because Muslims are certain that they have ousted the Christians from their homelands and killed many of them. The bombing of the Church of Our Lady of Deliverance attests to what they inherited from their parents of hatred against the Christians (infidels), and they pass it to their children.
- In general, Muslims may claim that these people do not belong to Islam at all, but this fact evades the bitter reality that says all or at least the majority of Muslims were against us before we left the country. On the other hand, Muslims accuse Christians of promiscuity as an attempt to marginalize them. For instance, these days a Christian lady has been nominated for the post of justice minister in Iraq. Rumors spread that that lady will produce sexual films. These false allegations forced that lady to appear in media outlets to dispel it. That is what we used to deal with as Christians—the distortion of our reputation to marginalize us.
- No one dared ever to launch such immoral claims under Saddam Hussein's rule. Saddam always brought Christians to his close circles in his palace for his knowledge of their loyalty and their dedication to work, especially in kitchens.

Note: This was the participant's views. The author is not responsible for thoughts that may appear to be un-conciliatory or judgmental.

Second Testimony

The situation of the Christians in Iraq can be divided into the pre-Saddam Hussein and later:

1. The period before overthrowing Saddam Hussein and his regime (up to 2003):
- I was born and raised in Baghdad where there was no difference between Muslims and Christians. The area where we lived was majority Christian. However, schools were state schools, and the majority of students were Muslims, and yet we did not feel any difference between Christians and Muslims. These schools were affiliated with the three Christian denominations (Catholic, Evangelical, and, Orthodox) that Saddam Hussein nationalized with all the private schools. Now, however, these schools are being demolished, and their sites are sold as land plots even though their title is still in the name of the churches.
- Under Saddam Hussein's regime, anyone who attacked Christians was to be punished. I remember when my son enrolled in the first-grade primary school (at the age of six). One day, he told us that his class teacher taught that the Christians are infidels (*kafir*). As parents, we went to school to complain to the teacher. She pleaded with us not to tell the principal because she would be punished and might lose her job.
- What a contradiction, the school was Christian, and the same school teaches that Christians are infidels. Another contradiction was that Saddam Hussein used to give money to the churches, especially in celebrating the anniversary of the establishment of the Ba'ath Party, but at the same time, the churches were monitored by the intelligence services. There was no religious freedom in the real sense of the word.

2. **The period after Overthrowing Saddam Hussein and his Regime (2003 to present)**
    - After the ousting of Saddam Hussein, political Islam (radical) prevailed. You may know that Iraq is divided into two major religious sects. Sunni is affiliated with Saudi Arabia and Shiite is affiliated with Iran. After 2003, both sects enforced strict religious tendencies towards Christians. Saddam Hussein was Sunni. Now Iraq has politically transformed from Sunni rule to Shiite rule.
    - Both sects became extremist against Christians.
    - The problems began with public killings the Christian community leaders and priests and bombing churches. Also, government members and their subordinate gangs began to seize Christian houses that were abandoned by their owners. Later the government agent members forced Christian owners to sell these houses at meager prices. For example, one time I went to pick up some stuff from my family's home, who was forced to evacuate, and I found out that a policeman was occupying the house. That policeman threatened me openly and said, "Christian properties are valid for us 'Muslims.'" The next day we had to sell it to a member of the government for half its value.
    - Some families found out that their houses had "not for sale" written on them. That meant no one would dare to come forward to buy it, because whoever did this would be killed.
    - It was pretty dangerous to walk down the street. So, we had to protect ourselves by wearing Islamic dress. Those who were not dressed like Muslims were to be killed, even if it was on the street. So life had become unbearable.
    - Overall, Muslims as individuals are friendly, but they become increasingly radical enemies when they turn to keep what the religion calls them to. Soon after Saddam's outset, we began to hear the mosques' loudspeakers claiming that Christians are

infidels (*kafir*) and to curse them in full view and hearing of everyone. Political Islam is the ultimate danger in the Middle East.

Relationship with Muslims here in Dayton:
- When we first came to Dayton as refugees in 2007, we were housed in a Muslim neighborhood because the organization was trying to bring all the refugees together. Our relationship with Muslims then was good. We helped them with interpretation and everything we could do, so much so that my son spent a whole night in hospital with a Muslim neighbor, and, as a result, he could not go to his college in the morning.
- Here is what we found in our relationship with Muslims. They do not want to keep healthy relations, but they return to us when they need our help. We all (Christians and Muslims) used to go to one of the refugee programs in one of the churches to help us settle, and once I heard someone say, "When do we get out of this place? I cannot bear it." He said, "to be in this place meant the church."
- Our family has a relationship with three Muslim families, but that does not mean that our relationship with them is strong or that they will change their minds about us as Christians.
- After all, life here in the States is not an easy one. We have to have a kind of solidarity and help each other. As Christians, we often lend a helping hand and love everyone, even if we do not visit them. They certainly know that.

Third Session
Go and Do Likewise

The previous two sessions were meant to help participants to examine themselves in relationships with the Other-different—namely our Muslim neighbors. It was profound that many of them had significant stories to share about their encounters with Muslims. Many of these stories compelled love of the Other-different, while some stories were tragic. This session is intended as a debriefing session during which participants would share and discuss what he or she can do to reach out to his/her brothers and sisters who are different than him/her. This session is about how participants can go beyond themselves to understand others and share the love of Christ with them. It might be helpful to think about the quote from Dr. Martin Luther King, Jr.: "People fail to get along because they fear each other; they fear each other because they don't know each other; they don't know each other because they have not communicated with each other."

Questions for discussion

1. How can we better connect with our Muslim neighbors? Jesus said to the lawyer, "Go and Do Likewise." Could you think of some practical ways, like visiting, inviting, giving help for something he/she needs, praying for, talking to, etc.?
2. How can we follow Jesus' teachings and show love for the Other-different? Remember that other-different might not be receptive to your ideas.
3. What can we do to bridge the gap between you and the Other-different in Dayton? Do you know any Mosque or Islamic community we can visit or invite to events?
4. Would you prayerfully tell us one or more creative way you can think of to reach out to your Muslim neighbor?

Based on the "Minorities Can Make A Difference" Session:

According to Berger the influence-ability or effectiveness and integration of any religious minority in its society depends on how the minority perceives themselves and their function, as well as how the majority perceives them.

1. How do we see ourselves religiously different from others?
2. In your opinion, how does the Other-different see us?
3. Do you believe as a small group we can make a difference. If so, how?

Third Session Analysis

Introduction

The researcher met with the Bible Group Study and reviewed the previous three lessons to remind participants of the goals of the field research. He introduced the aim and ultimate goals of the session: practical ways to reach out to our Muslim neighbors and how to bridge the social gap. The group has engaged in a dialogue about their past experiences and the obstacles that stand in the way of building meaningful relationships with their Muslim neighbors. The participants were very engaged and enthusiastic about the topics. In my assessment, the session was theoretically fruitful. The participants in this research are sincere and have positive attitudes about reaching out to their Muslim neighbors, but there are many questions about how to reach and approach them. How do we cross the psychological gap?

The group unanimously agreed that there are many barriers to building constructive and meaningful long-term relationships with our Muslim neighbors. The researcher gleaned from group discussions some stories that illustrate the barriers that some have personally encountered when dealing with Muslims in general. The stories should convey a broad spectrum of the problems:

- o The influence of some Mosques' teaching on Muslims: Muslims are taught that non-Muslims are "infidels" and therefore socializing with them is forbidden by the Sharia laws. For example, one group member shared with us the story that he has a Muslim neighbor who, despite being married to an American lady, has never greeted the group member nor shaken hands with him just because his family is Christian. Many times the member has extended his hand to him, and his Muslim neighbor refused to reciprocate.

- The culture divide between men and women in Islam: One member of the group is a professor at a major university, and he encounters Muslims on a daily basis. He shared with the group that he has invited many Saudi students to his home for meals and even hosted graduation parties for some. He sadly mentioned that once he hosted a graduation party for a Saudi student. That student did not invite any of his Saudi friends. When the professor asked him about it, the student immediately said, "I trust you looking at my wife since you are Christian, but I do not trust them." This is an illustration of the cultural divide between men and women in Islam and the mistrust that exists among them. The Saudi student proceeded to say that he has not forgiven his own brother because five years ago he made a deliberate move to see his wife without her hijab.

- The Christian barriers: Some Christians are heavy handed when dealing with Muslims. They immediately wanted to convert them, or otherwise they want nothing to do with them. One of the group members who has close ties with many Muslim ladies and who is working on her Ph.D. at Wright State University shared her views about missteps Christians commit. She pointed out that we must not look at Muslim neighbors as "conversion objects," but, instead, we must consider them as humans who deserve our respect. Muslims are very sensitive to being looked at as targets of witnessing and conversion.

- The Islamic culture: In Islam, families are united and respectful of elders. Senior members can carry great authority over the extended family, making it very hard for one member to go against the rest in deciding to interact with a Christian fellow. In addition, the cultural standing of women in Islam can hinder personal visits and hence the establishment of close family relationships.
- Honor and shame is in the heart of Islam. If one member of a family becomes a Christian, it can bring great shame on the rest, who have failed in their duty to keep the family together in Islam.

Next the group addressed some practical steps that can be taken to bridge and close the gap between us and our Muslim neighbors. Our Muslim neighbors need Jesus in Dayton as much as anywhere else in the world. Muslims are on the rise in the West. Look at this in a positive way. They are coming to us, and we do not have to go to them to introduce them to the Gospel. Instead of trying to build walls to protect ourselves from them, we try to build bridges that will help us reach out to them. Instead of being outraged at Muslim migration, we should seize this incredible opportunity and get to know and reach out to them. There are seven mosques in the greater Dayton area that we might visit. However, before doing so, a serious preparation must take place, and we must build trust between us and them in advance.

The researcher assumes it is easier to socialize with Western Muslims rather than Arabs. There are many strategies that we could use to reach out to them. Below I will list the group top four:

1) Try to learn as much about them, and, most importantly, try to draw on the positive things that the Quran mentions about the Bible.
2) Try to be their long-term friends. Plan a block party on your street and invite them and introduce them to other Christians. Be supportive when tragedy strikes them by visiting their

Mosque or Islamic Center and making donations to them in the name of your church. We share many commonalities, and they look at us as the people of the Book.
3) Try to patronize their businesses.
4) Have spiritual conversations with them by talking about what you believe and showing genuine concern for their families. Ask what they believe in and try not to be judgmental but critically supportive.

Next the group elaborates on how can we make others see Jesus through us. Christians are known for their unconditional and unlimited love for others. How can we claim that we love Jesus and not love or be indifferent towards others? How we love others, particularly other Christians, reveals how we love God. Jesus' teachings translate to this: How we can hate people and reach out to others at the same time? Again, the professor in the group shared that many of his Saudi students continue taking his courses for years, and most ask him to serve on their Ph.D. committees. He has asked many of them about this, and all of them answer, "Because you respect us." Some have bluntly said, "Because you are Christian and always show love and concern toward us." This is in spite of the fact that there is one Arabic-speaking Muslim professor and two other Muslims in the same department.

However, the participants are well aware of the challenges of encountering Muslims and are cautious not to set high expectations. One member of the group shared a story of an American friend of his. The American Christian friend went to a Mosque in the Dayton area to reach out to the Sheik. He was welcomed the first time around, but then the Sheik informed the American that, based on the feedback that he received from his congregation, he was not welcome to visit the Mosque again.

In conclusion the group recognizes the challenges and opportunities that are presented to them in reaching out to Muslims. The challenges are real and difficult to overcome, but they should not deter us from trying. The majority of the group is very enthusiastic to work on the differences, in theory. However, in practice, most members were faced with many obstacles and pushback from the respective communities, in general.

Conclusion

At the end of the late nineteenth and early twentieth centuries, Christians were actively participating in all walks of life politically and socially because the church had been active in society. Socio-politically active Christians in their countries were products of the missionary movement that began to emerge in the nineteenth century. Although these mission societies in some Middle Eastern countries such as Lebanon, Syria, and Egypt encountered strong resistance, they continued to engage in their societies, offering services such as mission schools, medical clinics, and other social services in villages and rural areas. In return, society was open to receiving education, health, and social services from them. That was the golden era when Christians participated in society as full citizens after the abolishment of *dhimma* laws and their implications.

The emergence of the radical Islamic movements in the late twentieth century raised prejudice and bigotry against Christians. Governments gradually marginalized Christians and used the movement for their own political benefit. Now, Christians are in danger of being pushed out of the Middle East entirely. Christians were receptive and became intimidated, contributing less and avoiding social life. In such an unhealthy environment of doubt, fear, and intimidation, Christians are incredibly vulnerable. The result has been for them to withdraw from society under the weight of righteous indignation. The history of relations between Christians and Muslims shows that both
were more open to the Other-Different when they developed nationalist feelings vs religious sentiment.

However, it has become clear to this author, that most of the participants in the questionnaires, the interviews, and the discussion are open to making social connections. On the other hand, it is clear that Muslims are struggling with evangelization phobia and still link the word *evangelization* with the word *crusade*. In addition to the focus group, the author has begun an ESL program through his church—teaching English as a second language—as well as an ASL program—teaching Arabic as a second language for Arab second generations. One of its goals is to engage the participants in social events such as Thanksgiving dinner, Christmas, etc. We arranged to sponsor a Thanksgiving dinner and have all the attendants come together. It was evident that Muslims are reluctant to participate in such social events.

In conclusion, this project has prompted a wave of self-reflection, research, and meaningful dialogue on the subject of loving the Other-Different. Fifty percent of the participants, at least, consider the matter seriously. There is a felt need to an ongoing interfaith dialogue project to take the issue to a new level of dialogue with the Other-Different. Indeed, we have just begun a long walk that will require enormous efforts of all people of good will to eliminate barriers and eradicate years of mistrust. We must join hands and walk together. It is exhausting to rebuild the trust, but the reward is worth a try.

APPENDIX A
Consent to Participate

APPENDIX A

CONSENT TO PARTICIPATE

Date ———————————

Dear ———————————

You are invited to participate in a study of ————————— ————————I hope you learn you learn ————————— —————————————. you were selected as a possible participant in this study because ——————————————————————— ———————————————————————————.

If you decided to participate please complete the enclosed survey. Your return of this survey is implied consent. The survive is designed to —— ——————————————————————————— . It will take about ———————————————————.

No benefits occur to you for answering the survey, but your responses will be used to ————————————— . Any discomfort of or inconvenience to your to you drives only from the amount of time taken to complete the survey.

Any information that is obtained in connection with this study and that can be identified was you will remain confidential and will not be disclosed.

Your decision whether or not to participate will not prejudice your future relationship with ——————————————— .If you decided to participate you are free to discontinue participation at any time without prejudice.

If you have any question please ask. If you have additional question later, contact ————————————————— .

Thank you for your time.

Sincerely, ——————————— Date ————

APPENDIX B

Project Registration

APPENDIX B

PROJECT REGISTRATION

The project was announced, and everyone in the group was encouraged to participate. While the researcher was announcing the next study session.

The objective of the research: "Bridging the Gap between Arab Christians and Muslims."

The problem revealed itself through one of the congregation's responses, meant as a joke. He said, "Between 'us' and 'them' a great chasm has been set." It was an indication of the depth of the problem before the project even began.

The day of the meeting, fourteen participants represented five Middle Eastern countries: Iraq, Lebanon, Jordan, Palestine, and Egypt. A registration and consent form was required to demonstrate each registrant's history, background, and willingness to participate in the study. The registration form asked for basic information: birthdate, country of birth, date of immigration, and reason of immigration, if possible. The participants were encouraged to answer, and the responses were kept confidential.

Name: Age: Country:
Date of immigration: ─────────────────────────────────
Reason of immigration: ───────────────────────────────

Please respond to all questions in this questionnaire. The information provided will help answer the question, "Why do Arab Christians not reach out to their neighbors?" It is the researcher's hope that this sample will be an accurate representation and a reflection of the attitudes, preferences, and opinions of Arab Christians in Middle East societies as well.[1]

---

[1] Louis M. Rea and Richard A. Parker, *Designing and Conducting Survey Research: A Comprehensive Guide* (San Francisco, CA: Jossey-Bass, 2014), 3.

APPENDIX C
Research Project Schedule

APPENDIX C

RESEARCH PROJECT SCHEDULE

October 5, 2018
Session One: Loving One's Neighbor: An Obligation, Duty, or Option.
The Biblical Foundation: Luke:10: 25-37, Lev.19: 33-34, and Deut.:10:17-19.
In addition to the registration form, the pre-session questionnaires were administered in person.
The objective of this questionnaire was to help the participant ponder his/her background relationship with the Other-Different as well as the overall relationship of the society in their countries of birth.
Task: was to complete the provided questions.

Ocober 19, 2018
Session Two: Minorities Can Make a Difference
The Biblical Foundation: The Power of Small Things
The objective of this questionnaire was to help the participant ponder on the minority influence in their countries of birth. Then the session was to give the participant the chance to ponder on the positive minority influence biblically, sociologically and historically.

November 2, 2018
Session Three: Go and Do Likewise
The Biblical Foundation: Luke 10: 37
The objective of this session was to help participants ponder on ways practical ways to reach out to their Muslim neighbors and bridge the social gap.

APPENDIX D
Questionnaires

PRE & POST-FIRST SESSION QUESTIONNAIRE,

PRE & POST-SECOND SESSION QUESTIONNAIRE

APPENDIX D

QUESTIONNAIRES

PRE-FIRST SESSION QUESTIONNAIRE

Name: _____

Please respond to all questions in this questionnaire. The information provided will help answer the question, "Why do Arab Christians not reach out to their neighbors?" It is the researcher's hope that this sample will be an accurate representation and a reflection of the attitudes, preferences, and opinions of Arab Christians in Middle East societies as well.[1]

1. Let's go back to the time before you left your country of origin. How would you rate the social participation between the Christian community, if it existed, with the majority neighbors in the country of your birth in your childhood?
   - None
   - Yes/weak
   - Yes/moderate
   - Yes/strong

2. How do you rate the relationship between Christians and Muslims in your home country now, compared to then?
   - Weaker than ever.
   - Moderate/ the same.
   - Stronger than ever.
   - Much stronger than ever.

3. Do you remember whether there was a relationship between your family and families of other religions during your childhood?

---

[1] Louis M. Rea and Richard A. Parker, *Designing and Conducting Survey Research: A Comprehensive Guide* (San Francisco, CA: Jossey-Bass, 2014), 3.

- o None
- o Yes/weak
- o Yes/moderate
- o Yes/strong

4. How many contacts with those of other religions from your childhood do you still keep in touch with today?
   - o None
   - o Yes, few and occasionally we meet.
   - o Yes, few and we have a strong relationship
   - o Lost my all contacts.

5. Do you remember any teaching in that period from the church about the other religion? If so, was it positive or negative?
   - o Not at all
   - o Yes, positive
   - o Yes, negative
   - o I do not remember.

6. It has been said that the rise of Islamic fundamentalist/Islamic revivalism began in the 1970s in many Middle Eastern countries, especially in Egypt.
   - o Disagree
   - o Agree
   - o Strongly agree
   - o I do not remember.

7. Do you remember any teaching in that period from the mosque/media attacking your Christian faith?
   - o Not at all
   - o Yes, positive
   - o Yes, negative
   - o I do not remember.

8. How much did these teachings/attacks affect or impact you and others?
   - o None
   - o Yes, strongly positive

- Yes, extremely negative
- I do not remember.

9. Can you name one or two of these affect/impact.
    - Positive impact(s): ....
    - Negative impact(s): ......
    - I do not really remember.
10. In your assessment, why?
    - Positive impact(s): ....
    - Negative impact(s): ......
11. Did you feel that you were treated the same as your Muslim colleagues in school at the time?
    - Never felt that way
    - Sometimes felt that way
    - Always felt that I was treated like my Muslim colleagues
    - It is hard to tell.
12. Did the Christian community enjoy the freedom to worship freely in your country like the majority?
    - No, we do not.
    - Yes, we do.
    - Enjoy limited freedom.
    - I am not sure.
13. Do you believe that your educational rights were violated?
    - No
    - Yes
    - I am not sure
14. What about the language curricula in your country: did you ever have to recite the Qur'an as part of your Arabic language curriculum and literature?
    - No, I did not.
    - Yes, I did.
15. What about the Christian history of your country: did you ever have to study Christian history as a part of your history curriculum?

- o   No, I did not.
- o   Yes, I did.

16. Have you, your family, or one of your close relatives ever experienced harm, mistreatment, or threats in the past?
    - o   No, I did not.
    - o   Yes, I did.
    - o   I would not call it that.

17. If yes, do you believe that harm or mistreatment was a result of your religion?
    - o   No, I did not.
    - o   Yes, I did.
    - o   I did not have it but overall I feel some sort of injustice.
    - o   I would not call it.

18. Have you or a family member ever been accused, charged, arrested, detained, interrogated, convicted and sentenced, or imprisoned with false charges because of your faith?
    - o   Yes, I did.
    - o   No, I did not.
    - o   I did not have it but overall I feel some sort of injustice.

19. Have you ever felt bitterness/resentment toward your neighbor Muslims in your childhood?
    - o   Yes, I did.
    - o   No, I did not.
    - o   I did not have it but always I feel unfair.

POST-FIRST SESSION
QUESTIONNAIRE

Name: _____

Please respond to all questions in this questionnaire. The information provided will help answer the question, "Why do Arab Christians not reach out to their neighbors?"

Questions about the good neighbor.

1. After you attended this Bible Study Session, who would you say is your neighbor?
   - Family members
   - Christian community
   - Anyone who needs my help

2. Have you seen this teaching of loving your neighbor put into action in your community before? Stories if possible.
   - No, I haven't had the chance.
   - Yes, I have.
   - I am not sure.

3. How do you classify the figures involved in the Good Samaritan parable according to their knowledge/act of the law? Robber, Priest/Levite (considered the highest religious rank), Samaritan (considered pagan and impure).
   - The highest applied the law of love the neighbor.
   - The least applied the law of love the neighbor.
   - Who did not know the law.

4. In Jesus' parable, who got the praise? And why?
   - He who knows the law and teaches it.
   - He who applies the law even if he does not know it.
   - He who violates the law.

Why? _____

5. How do you see the Other-Different religious and least knowledgeable of the law in the parable act, namely the Samaritan?

    a. He acted according to the law and fulfilled the "love your neighbor" commandment.
    b. He applied the law/scripture.
    c. He did what is simply required by the law.
6. How do you see Christ's teaching about loving your neighbor?
   - Realistic.
   - Impossible.
   - I do not know.
7. In light of this session, in your opinion, why do we as Arab Christians not reach out to Muslims, even though we know the scripture?
   - _____
   - _____
8. In your opinion, what does it mean to you to be neighborly?
   - _____
   - _____
9. Why is it important for us to be willing to be in relationship with the Other-Different?
   - _____
   - _____
10. Did the biblical teaching of the Good Samaritan change your process of thinking about the concept of your neighbor?
    - Yes.
    - No
    - I will think about that.
11. Please indicate, if possible, one or more neighborhood social activities that you could do to connect with your neighbors in the future.
    - _____

End.

PRE-SECOND SESSION QUESTIONNAIRE

Name: _____

The information provided is confidential.

1. In your estimation, can a minority influence the actions of a majority?
   - I agree   why? _____
   - I disagree   why? _____
2. Inspired by Jesus' parable on the power of little things, and based on the examples provided for the changes have happened in the world, do you think, as a minority, we can provoke the majority to change their attitudes in our Arab societies?
   - No. I don't think so.
   - Yes, I think so.
   - Our influence is weak.
   - Our societies are not changeable.
3. In you are in agreement with the previous statement, how can a minority influence the majority attitude? What do you say to someone who claims that it is impossible for the minority to make a difference in Muslim society? Give examples if you could.
   - _____
   - _____
4. Has your perspective changed as a result of your participation in this project?
   - Yes
   - No
5. What do we need to make the desired difference in our Arab societies?
   - _____

6. Would you indicate, if possible, one or more of neighborhood activities that you could do to connect with your neighbors in the future?

POST-SECOND SESSION
QUESTIONNAIRE

Name: _____

The information provided is confidential.

7. In your estimation, can a minority influence the actions of a majority?
   - I agree   why? _____

   - I disagree   why? _____

8. Inspired by Jesus' parable on the power of little things, and based on the examples provided for the changes have happened in the world, do you think, as a minority, we can provoke the majority to change their attitudes in our Arab societies?
   - No. I don't think so.
   - Yes, I think so.
   - Our influence is weak.
   - Our societies are not changeable.

9. In you are in agreement with the previous statement, how can a minority influence the majority attitude? What do you say to someone who claims that it is impossible for the minority to make a difference in Muslim society? Give examples if you could.
   - _____
   - _____

10. Has your perspective changed as a result of your participation in this project?
    - Yes
    - No

11. What do we need to make the desired difference in our Arab societies?
    - _____

12. Would you indicate, if possible, one or more of neighborhood activities that you could do to connect with your neighbors in the future?
   ○ ───────────────────────────────
   ○ ───────────────────────────────

End.

APPENDIX E

Individual Interviews And Devotionals

APPENDIX E

Individual Interviews

The researcher solicited the participants' input about these two questions:
- When, in your assessment, does social disintegration happen in our Middle Eastern countries? Why?
- What are the underlying reasons for that social disintegration?
- How can we get over this social disintegration again?
- The minority was able to bring about many social changes in Egypt in the 20th century. For instance, because of the impact of the church and the American missionaries, Egyptian Christians were able to stop running their private businesses on Sundays. Christians did not swear on the Bible in court. Christians started the liberation of slaves movement, and Christians were able to change the village market from Sundays to another day during the week in some villages.
- Can you please share a story or situation in your diary as an example of minority influence on the majority? And why?

BIBLIOGRAPHY

Adeyemo, Tokunboh, ed. *Africa Bible Commentary*, 1st edition. Grand Rapids, MI: World Alive Publishers, Zondervan, 2006.

Ahern, Annette Jean. *Berger's Dual-Citizenship Approach to Religion. American University Studies* Series, 202. New York, NY: Peter Lang Publishing Co., 1999.

Ambrose, Colin M. "Desiring to be justified: An Examination of the Parable of the Good Samaritan in Luke 10:25-37." *Sewanee Theological Review* 54, no. 1 (2010): 17-28.

Ashford, Paul. "Social Psychological Dimensions in Environmental Response." Guildford, England: University of Surrey, 1994.

Attia, Ayad S. "The Impact of the American Mission Schools on Egyptian Education from the Mid-Nineteenth to the turn of Twentieth Century" Master's thesis. Cairo, Egypt: The Evangelical Theological Seminary in Cairo, 2013.

Avakian, Sylvie. "The Turn to the Other: Reflections on Contemporary Middle Eastern Theological Contributions to Christian-Muslim Dialogue." *Theology Today* 72, no. 1 (April 2105): 77-83.

Azumah, John Alembillah. *The Legacy of Arab-Islam in Africa: A Quest for Inter-Religious Dialogue*. London, UK: Oneworld Publications, 2014.

Bailey, Betty Jane and J. Martin Bailey. *Who Are the Christians in the Middle East*. Grand Rapids, MI: Eerdmans, 2003.

Bailey, Kenneth. *Through Peasant Eyes: More Lucan Parables, their Culture and Style*. Grand Rapids, MI: Eerdmans, 1980.

Basic, Dennis. *Rights of Minorities in Islam form Dhimmis to Citizens.* ebook. 1-56: HR in Islam-Lecture 6 S.pdf, 2015. http://depts.washington.edu/.

Bauckham, Richard. "The Scrupulous Priest and the Good Samaritan: Jesus' Parabolic Interpretation of the Law of Moses 1." *New Testament Studies* 44, no. 4 (October 1998): 475-489.

Baum, Wilhelm, and Dietmar W. Winkler. *The Church of the East: A Concise History. volume 1 of Central Asian Studies.* London, UK: Routledge Curzon, 2003.

Beaumont, Mark I. *Christology in Dialogue with Muslims: A Critical Analysis of Christian Presentations of Christ for Muslims from the Ninth and Twentieth Centuries.* Eugene, OR: Wipf and Stock Publishers, 2011.

Ben-Hayyim, Zeev. "The Samaritan Pentateuch and the Origin of the Samaritan Sect." *Biblica* 52, no. 2 (1971): 253-255.

Berger, Peter. *A Rumor of Angels: Modern Society and the Rediscovery of the Supernatural.* Garden City, NY: Anchor Books, 1970.

Betts, Robert Brenton. *Christian in the Arab East: A Political Study.* Athens, Greece: Lycabettus Press, 1975.

Block, Corrie. *The Qur'an in Christian-Muslim Dialogue: Historical and Modern Interpretations.* London, UK and New York, NY: Routledge, 2013.

Bostom, Andrew G. "The Muslim Mainstream and the New Caliphate." http://www.americanthinker.com/articles/2007/04/the_muslim_mainstream_and the.html.

Blomberg, Craig L. *Interpreting the Parables.* ebook. Intervarsity Press, 2012.

Bromiley, Geoffrey W., ed. *The International Standard Bible Encyclopedia*, Revised ed. Vol. 4. Grand Rapids, MI: Eerdmans Publishing, 1988.

Brunner, Emil. *Faith, Hope, and Love*. Philadelphia, PA: The Westminster Press, 1956.

Budge, E. A. Wallis. ed. *The Book of Governors*. Vol. 2. By Thomas Bishop of Marga. London, UK: K. Paul, Trench, Trübner & Company, Limited, 1893. The University of Michigan, Digitized Apr 13, 2006.

CBN News. June 23, 2016. "Christians and Muslims - How to Bridge the Gap." http://www1.cbn.com/cbnnews/world/2016/june/christians-and-muslims-how-to-bridge-the-gap.

Chilton, Bruce D. Darrell L. Bock and Daniel M. Gurtner. Editors. *A Comparative Handbook to the Gospel of Mark: Comparisons with Pseudepigrapha, the Qumran Scrolls, and Rabbinic Literature*. Vol. 1 *The New Testament Gospels in Their Judaic Contexts*. Leiden, Netherlands: Brill, 2010.

Clark, Patrick M. "Reversing the Ethical Perspective: What the Allegorical Interpretation of the Good Samaritan Parable Can Still Teach Us." *Theology Today* 71, no. 3 (October, 2014): 300-309.

Coakley, J. and Sterk, A. ed., (2012). *Early Medieval Christianity in Asia. 45*. Apology of Patriarch Timothy of Baghdad before the Caliph Mahdi. in: *Readings in World Christian History: V1: Earliest Christianity to 1453*, 11th ed. Maryknoll, NY: Orbis, 231-242.

Collins, Kenneth J. "John Wesley's Engagement with Islam: Exploring the Soteriological Possibilities in Light of a Diversity of Graces and Theological Frameworks" Originally Presented Collins, Kenneth J. "John Wesley's Engagement with Islam: Exploring the Soteriological Possibilities in Light of a Diversity of Graces and Theological Frameworks" (published in The Path of

Holiness, Perspectives in Wesleyan Thought in Honor of Herbert B. Mcgonigle, edited by Joseph Cunningham [Lexington, KY: Emeth Press, 2014], 175–96).

Crossan, John Dominic. *In Parables: The Challenge of the Historical Jesus.* New York, NY: Harper & Row Publisher, 1973.

Derby, Josiah. "The Third Commandment." *Jewish Bible Quarterly* 21 (1993): 24-27. *Old Testament Abstracts.*

Donahue S.J., and John R. "Who Is My Enemy? The Parable of the Good Samaritan and the Love of Enemy." *The Love of Enemy and Nonretaliation in the New Testament,* Willard M. Stwartley, ed. Studies in Peace and Scripture. Institute of Mennonite Studies. 1st ed. Louisville, KY: Westminster/John Knox Press, 1992, 137–156.

Encyclopedia of the Modern Middle East and North Africa. "Dhimma." *Encyclopedia.com.*

Encyclopedia Britannica. https://www.britannica.com

English Oxford Living Dictionaries. "Umma". *The Online Oxford Dictionaries..* https://en.oxforddictionaries.com

Farmer, William R. ed. et al. *The International Bible Commentary: A Catholic and Ecumenical Commentary for the Twenty-First Century.* Collegeville, MN: Liturgical Press, 1998.

Francians, Pope. "General Audience: On the Parable of the Good Samaritan-ZENIT- English." April 27, 2016. https://zenit.org/articles/general-audience-on-the-parable-of-the-good-samaritan/

Gagnon, Robert A J. "A Second Look at Two Lukan Parables: Reflections on the Unjust Steward and the Good Samaritan." *Horizons in Biblical Theology* 20, no. 1 (June 1998): 1-11.

Ganz, Marshall. "Why David Sometimes Wins: Strategic Capacity in Social Movements," in Jeff Goodwin and James M. Jasper, eds. *Rethinking Social Movements: Structure, Meaning, and Emotion.* Lanham, MD: Rowman & Littlefield, 2004. 177-198.

Glaser, Ida. "The concept of relationship as a key to the comparative understanding of Christianity and Islam." *Themelios* 11, no. 2 (1986): 57-60, 57.

Gonzalez, Justo L. *The Story of Christianity.* Rev. ed. Vol. 1, The Early Church to the Dawn of the Reformation. New York, NY: Harper One, 2010.

Grafton, David D. "Coptic-State Relations: Looking Back to Look Forward." In *The Cairo Journal of Theology* (2014): 5–24.

Griffith S. H. "John of Damascus and the Church in Syria in the Umayyad Era: The Intellectual and Cultural Milieu of Orthodox Christians in the World of Islam." *Hugoye: Journal of Syriac Studies* 11, no.2 (2011): 207-237.

Guirguis, Magdi. "Coptic researcher reflects on the late Pope Shenouda III," An interview, *the American University in Cairo press.*

———."Faith and Reason in Christian Kalam: Theodore Abu Qurrah on Discerning the True Religion" in *Christian Arabic Apologetics during the Abbasid Period (750-1258)*, eds by Samir Khalil Samir, and Jorgen S. Nielsen. LXIII. E. J. Brill: Leiden, Netherland, 1994. 1-43.

Habib, Rafik. al-Gaama'a al-Kebtiah bein al-Andmag wa al Ena'azal. Cairo, El-Shrouk. 2005.

Hackenburg, Clint. "An Arabic-to-English Translation of the Religious Debate between the Nestorian Patriarch Timothy I and the 'Abbāsid Caliph al-Mahdī." Master's thesis, The Ohio State University, 2009.

Hamilton, Ernest. "The Qur'anic Dialogue with Jews and Christians." *Chicago Theological Seminary Register* 80, no. 3 (1990): 24-38.

Harris, Ralph W, Stanley M Horton, and Gayle Garrity Seaver. *The New Testament Study Bible: Luke,* Springfield, MN: Complete Biblical Library, 1991.

Healey, John F. "The Syriac-Speaking Christians and the Translation of Greek Science into Arabic." Muslim Heritage. http://muslimheritage.com/article/syriac-speaking-christians-and-translation-greek-science-arabic.

Hertz, Todd. "Are Most Arab Americans Christian?" in *Christianity Today,* web-only (2003.) http://www.christianitytoday.com/ct/2003/marchweb-only/3-24-22.0.html.

Hughes, Barry E. "Love Your Neighbor? Christian/Muslim Relations as A Way of Fulfilling the Great Commandment." Dissertation, United Theological Seminary, 2005.

Human Rights Watch*,* August 21, 2013. "Egypt: Mass Attacks on Churches." www.hrw.org/news

Humanities: Religion & Spirituality the Meaning of Da'wah in Islam. *Islamic Supreme Council of America.* http://www.islamicsupremecouncil.org/understanding-islam/legal-rulings/44-what-is-a-fatwa.html.

Irvin, Dale T. and Scott W. Sunquist. *History of the World Christian Movement.* New York, NY: Orbis Books, 2001.

Jackson, Timothy Patrick. *Love Disconsoled: Meditations on Christian Charity. 7 Cambridge Studies in Religion and Critical Thought.* Cambridge, UK: Cambridge University Press, 1999.

Kass, Leon. *The Beginning of Wisdom: Reading Genesis.* Chicago, IL: The University of Chicago Press, 2003.

Kattan, Assaad Elias. "Christians in the Arab world: beyond role syndrome." *The Ecumenical Review* 64, no. 1 (March, 2012): 50-53.

Keck, Leander et. al., eds. *The New Interpreter's Bible, Complete Twelve Volume Commentary. Luke - John* vol. ix. Nashville, TN: Abingdon Press, 1995.

Khairi Abaza and Mark Nakhla. "The Copts and Their Political Implications in Egypt." October 25, 2005. https://www.washingtoninstitute.org/policy-analysis/view/the-copts-and-their-political-implications-in-egypt.

Kilada, William Soliman. "Christian-Muslim Relations in Egypt," in *The Vatican, Islam, and the Middle East*. Kail C. Ellis, O. S. A ed. New York, NY: Syracuse University Press, 1987.

Knitter, Paul F. "Islam and Christianity Sibling Rivalries and Sibling Possibilities." *Cross Currents* 59, no. 4 (Dec., 2009): 554-570.

Kritzeck, James. "Islam and Christian unity." *Worship* 33, no. 8 (August, 1959): 477-481.

Malek, G. N. "Christian-Muslim dialogue." *Missiology* 16, no. 3 (July, 1988): 281.

Marshall, I. Howard. *The Gospel of Luke. A Commentary on the Greek Text. (NIGTC)*. Grand Rapids, MI: Eerdmans, 1997.

Mazamisa, L. W. *Beatific Comradeship: An Exegetical-Hermeneutical Study On Lk 10: 25-37*. Kampen, Netherlands: J. H. Kok, 1987.

McCall, Bradford. "Emergence Theory and Theology: A Wesleyan-Relational Perspective." *Wesleyan Theological Journal* 44. no. 2 (December, 2009): 189-207.

McCann, Samuel A. "The Political Marginalization of Arab Christians in the British Mandatory Period." *College of Arts & Science*

University of Oklahoma. (December 7, 2015) www.ou.edu/cas/history/images/docs/13_McCann_Marginalization.pdf.

Meier, John P. *A Marginal Jew: Rethinking the Historical Jesus.* New Haven, CT: Yale University Press, 2016.

Mingana, Alphonse. *The Apology of Timothy the Patriarch before the Caliph Mahdi,* in Wood Brooke Studies, Christians in Syriac, Arabic, and Garshuni edited and translated with critical apparatus. Vol. 2. 26-338.

Mitri, Tarek. "Christians in the Arab world: minority attitudes and citizenship." The *Ecumenical Review* 64, no. 1 (March 2012): 43-49.

———. "Christians-Muslim Relations in the Arab World," in *My Neighbor is Muslim: A Handbook for Reformed Churches.* John Knox Series no. 7. Geneva, Switzerland: John Knox, 1990.

Muck, Terry C. "Missio-logoi, interreligious dialogue, and the parable of the Good Samaritan." *Missiology* 44, no. 1 (January, 2016): 5-19.

———. "The Third Moment of Muslim Witness: John Wesley Had It Right," *A Theta Phi Lecture, Asbury Journal* 61, no. 1 (Spring, 2006): 83-95.

Nolland, John. *Luke 9: 21-18: 34, World Biblical Commentary, V35B,* David Hubbard and Glenn W. Barker ed. Dallas, TX: Word Books Publishers, 1993.

Nwaiwu, Francis O. *Inter-religious Dialogue in African Context.* Rome, Italy: Pontificia Universitas Urbaniana, 1989.

Norris, Frederick W. "Timothy I of Baghdad, Catholicos of the East Syrian Church, 780-823: Still a Valuable Model." International Bulletin of Missionary Research 30, no. 3 (July 1, 2006): 133-136.

Olson, Mark K. "John Wesley's doctrine of sin revisited." *Wesleyan Theological Journal* 47. no. 2 (Fall, 2012): 53-71.

Orr, James, M.A., D.D. General Editor. "Entry for 'LAWYER.'" *International Standard Bible Encyclopedia*. 1915.

Oord, Thomas Jay. "Essential Kenosis: An Open and Relational Theory of Divine Power: Between Voluntary Divine Self-Limitation and Divine Limitation by Those External to God." *American Academy of Religion, Open and Relational Theologies unit*, San Diego, CA. (November, 2007.)

Papaconstantinou, Arietta. "Between *umma* and *dhimma*: The Christians of the Middle East under the Umayyads." In *Annales islamologiques* 42 (2008): 127-56.

Parshall, Phil. "Applied spirituality in ministry among Muslims." *Missiology* 11, no. 4 (October, 1983): 435-447.

Patte, Daniel, ed. *Global Bible Commentary: Luke*. Nashville, TN: Abingdon Press, 2004.

Post, Stephen G. *A Theory of Agape: On the Meaning of Christian Love*. Lewisburg, PA: Bucknell University Press, 1990.

Rahner, Karl. *The Love of Jesus and the Love of Neighbor*. trans. Robert R. Barr. New York, NY: Crossroad, 1983.

Rea, Louis M. and Richard A. Parker. *Designing and Conducting Survey Research: A Comprehensive Guide*. San Francisco, CA: Jossey-Bass, 2014.

Reynolds, Gabriel S. *A Muslim Theologian in the Sectarian Milieu: 'Abd Al-Jabbār and the Critique of Christian Origins* in *Islamic History and Civilization* 56. Leiden, Netherlands: Brill, 2004.

Rhodes, Bryan D. "John Damascene in Context: An Examination of 'the Heresy of the Ishmaelite' with Special

Consideration Given to the Religious, Political, and Social Contexts During the Seventh and Eighth Century Arab Conquests." Master's thesis, Liberty Baptist Theological Seminary, Lynchburg, VA, 2009).

Rodkinson, Michael Levi, Isaac Mayer Wise, and Godfrey Taubenhaus. *Babylonian Talmud: Original Text, Edited, Corrected, Formulated, and Translated into English*. V. vii. Boston, MA: Talmud Society, 1918.

Rowberry, Ryan and John Khalil, *A Brief History of Coptic Personal Status Law*. 3 Berkeley J. Middle East. & Islamic Law. 81 (2010).

Rubin, Barry, *Islamic Fundamentalism in Egyptian Politics*. New York, NY: Palgrave Macmillan, 2002.

Samir, Samir Khalil. "The Earliest Arab Apology for Christianity (C. 750)." In *Christian Arabic Apologetics during the Abbasid Period (750-1258)*, eds. Samir Khalil Samir, and Jorgen S. Nielsen. LXIII. E. J. Brill: Leiden, Netherland, 1994, 57–114.

———. *The Church in the Shadow of the Mosque: Christians and Muslims in the World of Islam*. Princeton, NJ: Princeton University Press, 2012.

Schaeffer, Francis. *The Mark of the Christian*. Abridged Edition. http://www.ccel.us/schaeffer.html.

Scott, Bernard Brandon. *Hear Then the Parable: A Commentary on the Parables of Jesus*. Minneapolis, MN: Fortress Press, 1989.

Sider, Ronald J. *Rich Christians in an Age of Hunger: A Biblical Study*. Downers Grove, IL: Intervarsity Press, 1977.

Snodgrass, Klyne R. *Stories with Intent: A Comprehensive Guide to the Parables of Jesus*. Grand Rapids, MI: Eerdmans, 2008.

Starkey, Peggy. "Agape: A Christian Criterion for Truth in the Other World Religions." *International Review of Mission* 74, no. 296 (1985): 425-463.

Stott, John R. W. *Christian Mission in the Modern World: What the Church Should Be Doing Now.* Downers Grove, IL: Intervarsity Press, 1975.

Strong's Concordance with Hebrew and Greek Lexicon, https://biblehub.com. Online Bible Study Suite

Szukalski, John A. *Tormented in Hades: The Rich Man and Lazarus (Luke 16: 19-31 and Other Lucan Parables for persuading the Rich to Repentance).* Eugene, OR: Wipf and Stock Publisher, 2013.

Tannehill, Robert C. *The Narrative of Luke-Acts: A Literary Interpretation, Volume 1 the Gospel According to Luke.* Philadelphia, PA: Fortress Press, 1986.

Thiselton, Anthony C. "Parables as language-event: some comments on Fuchs's hermeneutics in the light of linguistic philosophy." Scottish Journal of Theology 23, no. 4 (November 1970): 437-468.

Thomas Bishop of Marga. *The Book of Governors*, Edited by Ernest Alfred Wallis Budge. *Google ebooks.* Vol. 2. London: K. Paul, Trench, Trubner & Company, 1893. Digitized by the *University of Michigan*, April 13, 2006.

Timothy I and Al-Mahdi: The Great Debate. (2013). [Blog] *ACU blog.* http://blogs.acu.edu/jks07b/files/2013/04/BIBH-674-Timothy-I.docx.

Tillman, J. Jeffrey. "Sacrificial agape and group selection in contemporary American Christianity." *Zygon* 43, no. 3: 541-556.

Vatican II. *Pastoral Constitution on the Church in The Modern World — Gaudium et Spes.* 7 (Dec. 1965 https://www.ewtn.com/library/councils/v2modwor.htm.

Volf, Miroslav, Ghazi bin Muhammad, and Melissa Yarrington, edit. *A Common Word: Muslims and Christians on Loving God and Neighbor*. Grand Rapids, MI: Wm. B. Eerdmans Publishing, 2010.

Wessels, Antonie. *Arab and Christians? Christians in the Middle East*. Kampen, Netherlands: Kok Pharos Publishing House, 1995.

Yeor, Bat. *The Decline of Eastern Christianity Under Islam: From Jihad to Dhimmitude: Seventh-Twentieth Century*. ebook. 1st ed. Madison, NJ: Fairleigh Dickinson University Press, 1996.

Youm'7 Newspaper. Interview with Dr. Andrea Zaki Stephanous, the President of the Protestant Community of Egypt. http://www.Youm'7.com/story/2018/4/7.

Made in the USA
Columbia, SC
26 October 2024